THE ART OF
SINGING
ON STAGE and in the STUDIO

THE ART OF

SINGING

ONSTAGE and in the STUDIO

UNDERSTANDING THE
Psychology, Relationships, AND Technology
IN PERFORMING AND RECORDING

JENNIFER HAMADY

Hal Leonard Books
An Imprint of Hal Leonard Corporation

Published in 2016 by Hal Leonard Books
An Imprint of Hal Leonard Corporation
7777 West Bluemound Road
Milwaukee, WI 53213

Trade Book Division Editorial Offices
33 Plymouth Street, Montclair, NJ 07042

Permissions can be found on page 182, which constitutes an extension of this copyright page.

Printed in the United States of America

Book design by Lynn Bergesen

Library of Congress Cataloging-in-Publication Data

Names: Hamady, Jennifer, author.
Title: The art of singing onstage and in the studio : understanding the
  psychology, relationships, and technology in performing and
  recording / Jennifer Hamady.
Description: Montclair : Hal Leonard Books, 2016. | Includes index.
Identifiers: LCCN 2016004623 | ISBN 9781495050268 (pbk.)
Subjects: LCSH: Singing—Instruction and study. | Singing—Psychological
  aspects. | Sound recordings—Production and direction. | Music
  trade—Vocational guidance.
Classification: LCC MT820 .H225 2016 | DDC 783/.043—dc23
LC record available at http://lccn.loc.gov/2016004623

www.halleonardbooks.com

Contents

Part Two: Enter the Cast

Part Three: Mastering the Tools

Acknowledgments

My sincerest thanks . . .

To the entire Hal Leonard family, including John Cerullo and Marybeth Keating, for bringing this book to life, as well as Ben Culli and J. Mark Baker for helping to start the whole *Art of Singing* adventure. And to Mike Symonds, again, who is responsible for it all, thanks to the world's most serendipitous meeting and introduction.

To Rachel Kice for her wonderful friendship, her constant inspiration, and the beautiful and perfect painting she created for the cover of this book.

To John and Lucas . . . the loves of my life, my two best buddies, and the brightest stars in my sky.

And to you. For your e-mails, calls, and visits . . . for all of your wonderful questions, feedback, thoughts and ideas . . . Thank you for being so vulnerable and brave. For daring to not only take on finding your voices, but also discovering who you are. And for allowing me to be a small part of that incredible process. You all are the reason I wrote this book; you all are the reason I love doing what I do.

From the bottom of my heart, I thank you.

PART ONE

Setting the Stage

Introduction

I wrote my first book, *The Art of Singing*, to help singers find more joy and ease in their singing. Because at one time, I'd lost both.

When I went to college to study voice, what had always been an effortless process for me became technical and confusing. Try as I might, learning how to sing with my intellect rather than my body and its wisdom in charge just didn't work. My once largely automatic voice became something I had to think and overthink about, resulting in physical tension and frustration.

Looking around my program and, later, at my fellow singers in the studio and on tour, I noticed that I wasn't the only one struggling with this common approach. It seemed the more we all tried to learn, the less we were sure of.

With time, as well as some marvelous guidance, I came to realize that the way I had originally interacted with my voice was the right one, and that setting aside this precious, intuitive relationship would never generate lasting results. Only by once again trusting myself would I be able to allow my voice to develop as it always had . . . with it, rather than me, leading the way.

I thankfully found my way back to that wonderful place of trust, joy, and ease. And then became determined to help others to do the same.

Since the release of *The Art of Singing*, it has been such an incredible pleasure and privilege to connect and work with so many of you. Watching you discover and rediscover your voices has brought full circle the determination and hope that led me to write the book. I am so impressed and inspired by your experiences, and as always, look forward to hearing more about your adventures!

The Journey Continues

As I mentioned in the preface of *The Art of Singing*, learning about the voice is an ongoing exploration. There is always something new to discover, which I find myself doing on a regular basis.

This includes the expanding notion of what "singing" entails. While having a great voice is important, becoming a successful singer today requires much more than talent and training. Timing, whether we are business savvy, our ability to make critical decisions, and our tolerance for pressure and stress are far more important than many people realize when starting their careers (and even for some who have been in the industry for a long time).

There are many challenging issues singers encounter on the path to success, though I have found three to be particularly critical as well as problematic. In spite of their importance, however, they aren't always sufficiently addressed in training and, sometimes, they're not discussed at all.

This is a tremendous shame, because without the proper attention, any one of the three can (and often does) stop a career dead in its tracks. And in combination, they can destroy it altogether.

They are:

- Dealing with performance and performance anxiety effectively
- Managing technology onstage and in the studio
- Interacting with the men and women who facilitate that technology

The Voice, Performance, and Performance Anxiety

"I got to know my voice as a part of who I am, not a thing that I do. And because I have always seen the voice as an extension of myself, I am able to sing without having to think about it."

—Carrie Manolakos, Broadway Actress and Recording Artist[1]

I have always been fascinated by performance anxiety. It's incredible to think of the power it has to devastate our performances and our enjoyment of them, to say nothing of how slippery it can be when trying to address and resolve it. As both a performer and a coach, I've marveled at how hard people work to try to eradicate their fear, only to have it become an even more engrained fixture in their performances and careers.

What causes this discomfort, and why is it so pervasive and, in many cases, crippling? Why are some people able to blissfully share themselves and their talents with the world, while others are riddled with nervousness and even panic?

Most importantly, what can we *do* about it?

For starters, we need to back up and take a look at our fundamental beliefs about performance and the voice itself. We all know what the words mean, but our modern definitions and understandings don't honor what they are by design: *natural extensions of ourselves into the world.*

"Personally, I never thought of myself as a singer. This happy accident freed me from psychological considerations of any kind."

—Silvia Nakkach, Author, *Free Your Voice*[2]

The voice is not a thing that you have. It is a part of you. We are our voices and performance, by nature, is the act of sharing who we are.

Today, however, our culture puts far too much pressure on singing and performing, equating talent and success with personal value and worth . . . burdens they were never meant to carry.

Together, we'll explore how these faulty and exhausting ways of thinking came into being—as well as how to overcome them—so that we can reclaim the joy, freedom, and fearless self-expression that is the birthright of every one of us.

Stage and Studio Technology

"As singers, we get training in voice, auditioning, and, occasionally, some business in schools and conservatories. Yet knowing how to use today's technical tools is *the* thing that will make or break you."

—Vivian W. Kurutz, Singer and Playwright, NYC[3]

Over the years, I have become more and more concerned with how much trouble vocalists have with the technology they encounter onstage and in the studio. Microphones, headphones, and monitors . . . amplification, EQ, and compression . . . given the prevalence of these and countless other technical tools, you'd think that singers would be experts in dealing with them, or at the very least, familiar to some extent.

Unfortunately, this isn't always the case. While some take the time to learn about the technological aspects of their trade, the vast majority of singers spend years training and practicing without ever working with the gear they will have to deal with when it comes time to record and perform.

This is a huge problem. Not only is it unprofessional to be unprepared, it is also impossible to pursue a singing career, in any genre, without knowing how to manage these tools.[4] No matter how talented you are or how much money is behind you, if you're unable to rise to the technical challenges onstage and in the studio, you will not get very far.

Believe me, this is not an understatement. I've watched countless phenomenal singers stagnate professionally and even leave the business because they can't figure out how to deliver when using studio headphones and stage monitors. And I've seen just as many less capable singers get ahead because they can.

We're therefore going to go through all of the tools and concepts you must know in order to pursue a modern professional singing career, until you're as confident about recording and performing as you are singing in your voice lessons and rehearsal spaces.

Relationships: Singers, Producers, and Engineers

"Recording is of course a technical and musical process, but it is also about dealing with people. If you don't have, or can't acquire, interpersonal skills, you'll never become a recording engineer in a commercial studio."

—David Mellor, *Sound on Sound* magazine[5]

To tackle the issue of technology properly, we're not only going to look at the tools and concepts involved with stage and studio singing, but also at the men and women who facilitate both. This isn't just some feel-good courtesy; though it may come as a surprise to those of you who are new to the business, these relationships are capable of causing as many obstacles to success as a lack of knowledge about the gear. And not only for technicians; while David is speaking about engineers, his comment applies equally to singers.

What is it that can make these relationships so challenging? And why are they so important?

> *"Well the silver key's the back door, and the red one's for the front. And they left instructions for me in the den. And I'm meeting total strangers who will put this song together. It took every penny saved to get it done . . ."*
> —Risa Binder, Recording Artist/Songwriter, from *Nashville*[6]

For starters, many singers and engineers meet just before or on the day they'll begin working together. Often, a good deal of money is being spent on the studio, with management, label representation, and other pivotal career opportunities on the line. Live performances are also often make-or-break situations. Years of hard work, hope, and sacrifice have gone into preparing for these big moments. Given all that's at stake, the pressure is on and stress levels run high.

What's more, singers and technicians tend to come to these high-stakes tables with some pretty fixed notions about one another. For many reasons, including their lack of technical knowledge, singers are often anxious and insecure about recording and performing. And while engineers and producers may be sympathetic, over time they can become frustrated as well, particularly when great results aren't forthcoming. This frustration often leads vocalists to become even more insecure and uncomfortable with technicians, completing a circle of negative generalizations that can be hard to break.

Finally, performers and technicians tend to be two different types of people, who often have a hard time communicating with one another for a variety of reasons that we'll be exploring. Throw stereotypes and stress into the mix, and these misunderstandings frequently turn into mistrust and wariness, all of which makes it hard to work together the very moment they have to.

Whether or not you've ever stepped onstage or into a recording studio, you can likely relate at least somewhat to this scenario. After all, the relationships between singers, producers, and engineers are just that . . . *relationships*. In every aspect of the music business, and life, your ability to work well and communicate with other people is far more important than many realize. We're therefore going to take an in-depth look at these crucial but often neglected skills.

Of course, not everyone in the music business struggles with relationship issues. Many not only get along, but also attribute their success to the teamwork and creativity of their partnerships.

I've had the great fortune of being a part of this type of dynamic with producers and engineers on numerous occasions. During many sessions, we would talk about the knowledge gap and personal divide that often exist between singers and technicians, and the countless lost opportunities for high-quality performances, relationships, and fun. These conversations, along with the stories I hear almost daily about singers' disempowering relationships with their voices and debilitating performance anxiety, inspired me to get to the bottom of these conundrums, which have plagued the best vocalists and technicians for years.

This book is the result of that determination.

Bringing It All Together

At first glance, performance, technology, and relationships may seem like very different topics . . . so much so that I initially thought about addressing them individually. Certainly, each is a comprehensive conversation in and of itself!

Yet I've come to realize that part of the reason these issues continue to plague singers is because they are treated in isolation rather than presented as an integrated, singer-directed whole. And not only conceptually; when voice-related issues, technology, and interpersonal working dynamics are addressed, it tends to be from a *professional* standpoint, rather than from a holistic, *personal* one.

Understanding how to use a microphone may not matter in your private life, but the very personal traits of curiosity and openness are required to challenge yourself to learn and grow as a singer, particularly when it comes to unfamiliar and often intimidating areas like technology. And as we will discover throughout the book, your handling of performance anxiety and relationships onstage and in the studio are as influenced by who you are as by who you've become as a musician.

Dealing with these issues, then, is not just a matter of professional mastery. It's about acquiring skills that will also make you a more effective person.

We'll begin this journey by discussing the development of technology and the evolution of performance in our culture, including taking an in-depth look at the role of the voice throughout history, and the modern-day emotional, intellectual, and vocal impact of these changes on singers.

Next, we'll move on to the heart of the matter: reconstructing our experiences with performance and technology, as well as the relationships involved with both. We'll look at what hasn't worked and why, and explore how to transform the current dynamics into ones that will help to facilitate our best performances and interactions.

Finally, we'll take a comprehensive look at the recording and live audio technology itself, giving you the sense of empowerment and knowledge you need about the tools of your trade.

In *The Art of Singing*, we learned how to have healthy physical and emotional relationships with our voices. Now it's time to learn how to use those voices in the real world. Whatever your performance genre or technical medium, by book's end, you will know how to deliver confidently, comfortably, and consistently to any number of people, and to do so with the respect, support, and camaraderie of those with whom you're working.

A Few Things to Consider

Some of you might be particularly curious about one of these topics. Maybe you picked up the book wanting to get to the bottom of your struggles with performance anxiety, or to once and for all learn about the technology involved with singing.

Whatever brought you here, I encourage you to read all three sections. Don't let intimidation or a lack of seeming relevance stop you. The book presents a comprehensive and necessary package of information for modern singers. I'll say it again: today, technology is almost if not as important as the quality of your voice. And ineffectiveness in relationships with stage and studio personnel—as well as with managers, agents, and other industry professionals—can cause as many career stumbling blocks as performance anxiety and voice-related issues.

Trust me on this. Read the book cover to cover. You'll be glad you did.[7]

Generalizations

> "To draw the rule from experience, one must generalize; this is a necessity that imposes itself on even the most circumspect observer."
>
> —Henri Poincaré[8]

When it comes to technology, we're going to explore some stories and generalizations about how producers, engineers, and singers tend to interact with one another, in order to understand how we are perceived and what we can do better. If your hackles and defenses get raised, that's okay, and possibly even a good thing. No one flinches at a light touch; it's only when our skin is sensitive that contact becomes uncomfortable. The same is true for any sensitivities we haven't acknowledged and resolved when it comes to our personal and professional ways of being.

> "All generalizations are dangerous, even this one."
>
> —Alexandre Dumas[9]

For some, one area of sensitivity will be these stories and generalizations. Of course there are exceptions to every rule, and a book that seems to lump people together and highlight stereotypes can understandably be off-putting.

That said, there is a method to my madness. Not only is it impossible to look at each unique person and situation in a single book, but doing so also prevents us from exploring the tendencies that *do* exist, as well as their causes. What's more, focusing exclusively on people who've got it all figured out won't necessarily help those struggling get from where they are to where they want to be. That is why we're going to start by looking at what hasn't worked in order to learn and be able to implement what does.

Gender

> "When I started [as a recording engineer], I never saw being a woman as a disadvantage. I couldn't have, or I would have gotten nowhere. Only now, in hindsight, do I realize how high the hurdles were that I had to jump."
>
> —Lee Flier, Recording Engineer, Atlanta, Georgia[10]

While there is a relatively equal balance of men and women in singing and performing, far fewer women become producers and engineers. Thankfully, this has been changing in recent years, but the ladies are still lagging behind when it comes to the technical side of creating music.

No matter your thoughts on gender roles in the studio, onstage, or backstage, my use of "he" and "she" are interchangeable and arbitrary, just as they were in *The Art of Singing*.

Yet this time, they are arbitrary in spirit.

For the ease of reading, I will tend to refer to performers as "she" and to technicians as "he." I'm choosing to rely on what is easy and familiar so that our main focus can be on the content of what our characters are doing, rather than on whether they are men or women. And as we'll see in Part Two, this choice will also help to highlight and address a number of issues that exist onstage and in the studio because of gender.

Titles, Labels, and Names

> "I think it's so funny when I tell someone that I'm a singer and they ask whether I play an instrument. I always respond by saying, 'Yes! I just told you I did!'"
>
> —Nadia, Singer/Songwriter, NYC[11]

Is the voice an instrument? Are singers musicians? As Nadia points out, that depends on whom you ask and how you define the terms.

As far as I'm concerned, if you're in the habit of making music, you're a musician. Whether you sing or play the guitar, whether or not you have been trained or can read music make no difference. After all, some of the best musicians in the world have never taken a lesson. Pavarotti couldn't read music. Not being able to sight-read didn't stop Stevie Wonder from qualifying as a musical genius, and the inability to hear didn't prevent Beethoven from becoming one of the most accomplished and celebrated composers of all time.

That said, throughout the book I'll be using the word *musician* to refer to instrumentalists, as there are some important differences between how they and vocalists experience and interact with technology because of one critical distinction: singers' voices are *inside of their bodies*. By addressing the two separately, it will be easier to highlight the differences.

On the other hand, you'll notice that I'll be much more flexible when it comes to producers and engineers, often using the terms interchangeably or calling them both technicians. That's not to say that their roles and responsibilities are the same. Producers by definition are still the leaders and creative visionaries of the recording process, and engineers the technical wizards who bring those visions to life.

The greater ease and lower costs of recording these days, however, have led to an increasing amount of overlap between the two jobs, with many people now performing both. And while producers have always had to collaborate with singers, it is only recently that engineers, the once "silent knob turners," have taken a more interactive role in the recording process. As such, some of the larger communication challenges between singers and technicians tend to be with engineers, which is why I'll be using this term more frequently.[12]

Attention

Finally, though I respect singers and technicians equally, performers are my primary focus for a number of reasons. For starters, they're truly in need of this information. Why is their performance anxiety so ever-present and debilitating? Why does singing with monitors and headphones feel so unnatural? Why can it be such a challenge to communicate and get what they need in the studio? Even though I sincerely hope that everyone finds the book informative and helpful, my attention first and foremost while writing this book has been on the needs of performers.

Next and most importantly, the book is directed to singers because I am a singer. It's what I know; it is the perspective I come from. While many wonderful producers and engineers have helped me with this project, I am not writing a comprehensive guide to audio hardware and software or pretending to know the ins and outs of being a technician, either personally or professionally.

Instead, what I hope to contribute is a guide to help singers use and understand the tools that are an ever-increasing part of their performance lives, as well as the resources necessary for singers, producers, engineers, and others in the world of performance to communicate about them together.

What's more, I hope to inspire and encourage you to really listen to and learn from one another. No matter what you've been through, no matter what you think you're sure of, the good stuff is in partnership with other people . . . onstage, in the studio, and in life.

I hope you enjoy the book and find it helpful. Please feel free to share your thoughts and feedback, as well as news of all of the wonderful performances, recordings, and relationships that lie before you. I can be reached through my website, www.JenniferHamady.com.

CHAPTER ONE

The Emergence of Technology

A Different World

"One of the things that I hope to help my readers share is a sense of absolute astonishment that we're living in such an extraordinary age."
—Diane Ackerman, Author, *A Natural History of the Senses*[1]

Once upon a time, hard to imagine as it might be, YouTube, Facebook, and cell phones didn't exist. Neither did Apple. Or Microsoft. Or the Internet.

While it may be impossible for some of you to remember or envision life without e-mail, it was only in 1992 that it became available to the public. Since then, what was once unfathomable has become indispensable for most of us, forever altering our interactions with each other and our experience of the world.

And the trajectory of technology, even into the near future, is beyond imagining.

Equally baffling is a look at its past. Since the industrial revolution a mere two hundred years ago, the explosion and expansion of technological developments have in many ways made the previous few thousand years look like a standstill.

Thanks to the imagination and hard work of countless men and women, these developments have led to ideas and inventions that have shaped and continue to shape our world and the way we live in it. Medicine, travel, communication . . . construction, science, agriculture . . . even religion and art . . . there is hardly an industry that hasn't been touched by technology and, for the most part, vastly improved.

Technology in Music

The entertainment industry is no exception. The birth of amplification and transmission, both around one hundred years ago, heralded the ability to project the human voice beyond its physical capabilities. Radio waves soon carried these signals to the horizon and now, only a short time later, dazzlingly high-quality signals traverse the globe with the capability of reaching every human being on the planet.

We are not only able to hear people removed from our physical presence, but also to hear them dissociated from their physical selves. Recordings of speeches and songs live on, long after they've been captured by a recording device. This capturing, which also became possible around one hundred years ago, extends through film into the visual realm as well, allowing for a virtual, three-dimensional experience of another human being outside of the contexts of space and time, including long after they physically exist on the planet.

And technology hasn't stopped there. We can also experience people and performances in ways that never actually existed. In virtually every creative medium, technology allows us to edit, blend, and even create content that occurs to an observer—though it isn't—as a true and authentic experience. Airbrushing (cleaning up and refining visual images), splicing (cutting and pasting audio and video footage), and Auto-Tuning (correcting the pitch of voices and instruments) are only a few of the countless tools that are now available to manipulate photographs, videos, and recordings in ways that make them more appealing to the modern ear, eye, and taste.

A Bit of Perspective

> "We think it's totally normal for humans to go five hundred miles an hour and have computers in the palms of our hands, and know about dark matter. These things are quite majestic and extraordinary, but we take them for granted."
>
> —Diane Ackerman, Author, *A Natural History of the Senses*[2]

It's incredible when you stop and think about all that has happened within the last one hundred years or so! We've not only gone from a few local, scratchy radio channels, to black-and-white television, to satellites swirling in our atmosphere delivering endless amounts of perfected content to handheld devices anywhere in the world. We've also created cars, nuclear power, and airplanes. We've isolated and cured diseases. We've traveled to outer space and gathered visual and actual samples of distant planets and solar systems. We've unraveled and then cloned the DNA chain. We've walked on the moon.

In just a few generations, our entire world, the way we experience and interact with it, has radically altered.

Looking at a Lifespan

> "A man lives not only his personal life as an individual, but also, consciously or unconsciously, the life of his epoch and his contemporaries."
>
> —Thomas Mann[3]

When my aunt Josephine passed away a few years ago, she was one hundred years old. As such, she had the great fortune of living through many of our modern world's transformations, technological and otherwise.

Yet living through those transformations didn't allow her to feel their full impact. Time marches gradually, giving our minds and lifestyles a chance to adjust to new and shifting circumstances . . . even the most drastic and radical ones. While jumping from 1912 to today would provide a great deal of perspective, living through those years in real time kept my aunt from perceiving the enormity of the big picture.

The same is true for each of us. When the Internet came into being during my university days, it was a huge development. But as we already had television, CDs, beepers, cars, airplanes, and space travel, among other things, it didn't seem shocking to my friends or me (though it sure made researching and writing college papers easier!). From the perspective of having been born in 1974, while the Internet and e-mail were exciting, at the time they didn't seem all that radical.

Obviously, we now understand the monumental nature of both. And stepping back a few centuries, the profoundness of these and other changes becomes even clearer. From this vantage point, we are able to see that even the years from 1850 through today have been a revolutionary departure from the way things were before . . . the way they were for thousands and thousands of years.

An Analogy

Let's try to put this into a visual context. Imagine walking the length of one hundred football fields, only to arrive at a foot-thick wall jutting skyward at a hard, ninety-degree angle and extending into the sky well beyond your line of sight.[4]

If your walk is the duration of human history, the height of the wall an expression of the number of technological advances we've witnessed, its thickness the length of time in which those advances had been achieved, and the juxtaposition of the two the rate at which they came about (not gradual in the slightest!), you can begin to imagine the abruptness of the shift from a nontechnological to a technological world.

You may also start to sense the potential impact on human beings of such an immediate and radical departure from our previous course.

The Implications of Technology

Accommodation Versus Adaptation

Human beings, like all animals and plants, are adaptive. Meaning that over time, we're able to make the changes necessary to exist and thrive in any environment in which we find ourselves.

A good example is the "recent" losing of our sixth toe. As we began shifting some ten thousand years ago from barefoot scavengers to domesticated beings living in sheltered areas and protecting our feet, we eventually lost the need for the extra grip, power, and stability provided by the additional digit.

This didn't happen overnight. It wasn't as if shoes were invented and—poof!—the next generation was down a body part. Like all aspects of evolution, it was a very gradual process.

What we've seen with the emergence of technology in the last two hundred years, however, is something very different. Historically speaking, there has been nothing gradual at all about what has happened since the industrial revolution. In fact, it has been about as abrupt and radical as a change can get:

- After thousands of years to the contrary, thanks to the telephone and Internet, our senses are now unable to be fully activated in many of our interactions.

- Emotional responses, including the stress response, may for the first time be artificially triggered by manufactured, televised content, in addition to real-life exchanges.
- Vast amounts of digital information are presented at such rapid speeds— speeds at which they do not occur in nature—that much of it is impossible to intellectually recognize, much less cognitively process.

There are also a host of secondary implications of technology to consider. Multitasking, constant sensory bombardment and overload, diminished amounts of time and connection with nature and others, and greater exposure to electromagnetic frequencies all have an impact on our ways of being . . . an impact that is not yet fully understood or mitigated by coping mechanisms in our biology and brain chemistry.

Thankfully though, we human beings are as bright as we are resilient. Abrupt as the developments have been, we've demonstrated a tremendous ability to adjust to and even thrive in the face of all that has come about, as we have throughout history. Children and young people in particular seem able to step into our technology-filled and driven world and embrace it as if it were as much of a biological imperative as walking or eating.

Yet while we are able to adjust to advances in technology—some of us more so than others—we don't fully adapt to them.[5] There simply hasn't been enough time. What we do instead is accommodate these changes; we modify our ways of relating and behaving to the extent that we are able. And as we shall see in the next few chapters, we are only able to do so to a certain degree.

Our Current State

"Preceding generations have presented us with a highly developed science and technology, a most valuable gift which carries with it possibilities of making life free and beautiful to an extent such as no previous generation has enjoyed. But this gift also brings with it dangers to our existence as great as any that have ever threatened it."

—Albert Einstein[6]

Looking out my window at the Manhattan skyline, the buildings rising up into the sky and the planes flying over them, it's fun to try to imagine what this island looked like five hundred years ago. Hills, rivers, grass, and streams covered what was then primarily a collection of fields. What a different world we now live in.

And it's a great world! We're all aware of and thankful for the benefits of technology and progress. They are what have allowed me to digitally construct and distribute this book, to work with clients around the world through videoconferencing, and to fly to distant countries to give workshops.

While much has been gained, however, other things have been lost. There is a duality to everything, and technological innovation is no exception. The ingenuity that led to the invention of the space shuttle allowed for the creation of nuclear weapons. Airplanes and trains rival for top speeds, as do missiles and torpedoes. Developments in science create access to life and longevity as well as to disease and death.

Accommodation in Music

While not as dramatic or ethical, the duality of innovation also applies to music.

On one hand, audio technology provides a tremendous and awe-inspiring benefit to musicians and audiences alike. Consider the amount and types of beautifully recorded music that are available to us, as well as how often and easily we are able to hear them. Think about what access to music from around the world and throughout history provides for our education, awareness, spirits, and lives. Imagine the actual and digital instruments that have been invented for us to play and appreciate, and as a result, the endless amounts of music that anyone, anywhere can create and enjoy. For pleasure, historical preservation, study, and more, our ability to create, capture, and access music from every corner of the planet and throughout the ages is simply amazing.

At the same time, the inventions associated with recording and amplification in the last couple of hundred years have altered something—a way of being, living, and communicating that existed for thousands of years prior. In spite of our tremendous advances, we are more removed from the original purpose and experience of music creation and sharing that technology has sought to improve upon, as well as unable to cognitively and emotionally handle many of the gifts that it has provided.

In other words, in our effort to advance music through technology, we have also taken some very important things away. . . .

CHAPTER TWO

A History of the Voice

Back "then," before telephones, microphones, and recordings of any kind, interpersonal communication was very different. For starters, the voice could only travel as far as our physiology would allow. All verbal communication was delivered from mouth to ear—from person to person, or from person to a relatively small group—a limitation that was reflected in the size of communities for thousands of years. First migratory and later centralized around agriculture, small groups banded together, growing larger only as advances in farming and irrigation developed.

Communion and Community

During this time, the notion of community wasn't just a convenient concept or an ideal enforced by law. As with the vast majority of human history, it was created and cultivated out of necessity.

Think about it. There were no stores to pop into if you ran out of something, no newspapers to consult for weather reports. There was no radio, no history book, no school, and for a long time, no writing. Everything necessary for physical, emotional, educational, and spiritual sustenance was provided by the community.

And it was provided largely through the use of the voice:[1]

- Rituals brought people together, conferred power, and created partnerships.
- Ceremonies celebrated seasons and cycles of the moon, the hunting and sacrificing of animals, and the planting and harvesting of food.
- A people's past traveled through the present and into the future upon it; their history, wisdom, and traditions were captured, preserved, and shared in songs and stories.
- Birth, death, and life were honored through its usage.

Safety and Invitation

Ritual and ceremony also extended to those outside of the community. No matter the space between them, the distance between groups at times needed to be bridged and protected. Those who brought supplies to trade and barter and news from neighboring communities were welcomed in various vocal traditions, while the individual and group voice were used to warn and drive off those who sought to attack.[2]

Obviously a lot has changed since then! Yet while the world has altered and the spaces between us have been substantially reduced over the years, the essential nature and purpose of our communication remain largely the same. In person, on the phone, and over e-mail we too invite and warn. From near or far, as our ancestors did, we also defend ourselves and protect our territory, just as we extend our welcome to new friends and old, share our stories and histories, and celebrate the many milestones in our lives and in the lives of those we love.

What has changed over time is the voice with which we do so.

The Journey of the Voice

Just as the design and beauty of nature serve a purpose, our voices are the way they are for a reason. Imagine the plume of a peacock, the majesty of an orchid, or the intricate pattern of a lizard's skin or leopard's fur. Whether for safety, sustenance, or sex, nature evolves and exists in order to promote resourcefulness and to ensure self-preservation and perpetuation.

So too has the human voice evolved to elevate our chances for survival. Like all evolutionary tendencies, the development of ritual, ceremony, and even language were not by chance or for entertainment. They came about to strengthen communities and ensure their continued existence—a feat achieved by communication becoming as deliverable, accessible, and memorable as possible.

Deliverable

Rhythm, melody, and percussion have long been used by humans and animals to send and ensure the receipt of messages. Repetitive sounds, unique tones, and sharp vocalizations convey meaning with a conviction and clarity that leaves little doubt as to the communicator's intent.

Think of a bird, its entire body quivering with the power of its message. For thousands of years, humans were also reliant upon being able to use their voices so powerfully. Whether to evoke or express feeling in an intimate ritual, or to deliver a war cry, the ability to project the voice was a requirement, meaning that once upon a time we all had well-developed breath and support mechanisms, giving us effortless access to agility and range of both notes and emotion.

Accessible

Once language came into being though, particularly complex language, the sharp vocal distinctions necessary to discern meaning became more subtle as our words began to clarify our intent. That isn't to say that the creation of language led to a world of vocally muted monotone. While not as loud or rangy as a bird's call, melody and rhythm are still present and important in our speaking voices today, providing clues and access to a speaker's meaning.

As a demonstration, read any sentence on this page aloud, first seductively, then as a sharp command, and finally as a question. Even when your tone contradicts the meaning of the words you're reading, you'll notice that the "music" of each treatment has a tremendous influence over the way the words would be understood and experienced by the listener, as well as how you experience them as the speaker.

Memorable

Melody and rhythm not only help us to communicate with and understand one another. They also make our communications memorable.

Have you ever wondered how even the youngest of children so easily learn and recall nursery rhymes? Or how decades-old songs spring to the forefront of your mind at a casual mention, often in their entirety?

As powerful as language is today, it isn't the words that allow us to store and retrieve these songs from the depths of memory. It isn't even the rhyme schemes, though they definitely help.

It is the music—the melody—to which the words are linked that gives us such immediate and long-term access.

If you're uncertain of this connection, try hearing the following words in your mind *without* hearing a melody:

> "*Twinkle, twinkle, little star / how I wonder what you are*"[3]
>   and
> "*You may say I'm a dreamer / but I'm not the only one /
> I hope someday you'll join us / and the world will live as one*"[4]

Chances are that as your eyes scanned the words, the melody, or at least the rhythm of the melody, remained firmly attached.

Melody and Memory

> "I came to the conclusion a long time ago that the text of a song is the very specific idea—the point—and the music is the power behind that point. It's like a spear. The point can be sharp, but without the weight of the shaft behind it and the speed at which it's thrown, the point is powerless. Music empowers the ideas and makes them strong."
>
> —Jonathan Doyel, Director, Republic of Song[5]

This enduring connection is due to the way our memories are formed.

Think of the last time you smelled freshly baked cookies, cut grass, or the perfume or cologne of a loved one. Scents trigger vivid memories that not only bring back a recollection of our original encounter with them, but also make those recollections seem *real*. It doesn't matter how long ago a memory was formed, whenever you come across *that scent*, you are back there in time.

Music, like scent, has an equally powerful ability to capture, store, and evoke even early childhood memories, thanks in large part to various chemicals that fire in the brain when we sing or hear music (and to a slightly lesser extent, when we taste and see certain things,), particularly when the experiences are emotional in nature.[6]

Just as the details of our scent memories are carried forward, so too do the songs we learned long ago stay with us. This is why "Twinkle, Twinkle, Little Star" and "Imagine" fly instantly to the tips of our tongues, regardless of how many years it has been since we last heard or sang them.

The same is true of commercials, as advertising executives are well aware. See what comes to mind when you read:

- "I am stuck on Band-Aid brand 'cause Band-Aid's stuck on me"[7]
- "Oh, I'd love to be an Oscar Meyer wiener"[8]
- "Have a good night sleep on us . . . Mattress Discounters!"[9]

If these commercials were before your time (or not played in your country), try to recall any company's popular jingle without hearing the melody in your head. Or turn on your television and see how many commercials you are unable to sing along with.

Memory Versus Memorization

Here's another example of the link between music and memory, this one from my own life. Ask me to name the American presidents in succession, and I'll likely get stumped early into the double digits. Ask me to name each of the fifty states, however, and I can do so accurately, effortlessly, and even in alphabetical order.

This isn't due to some fascination with US geography. Rather, it's thanks to a song I learned in elementary school that put a melody to the alphabetized states. After a few times singing it through, the song—and the states-turned-lyrics—were firmly and forever locked in my mind.

If only all of my schooling had been put to a tune!

Short-term Versus Long-term Memory

Without the music, learning and attempting to recall the states alphabetically would have been a very different experience. Why? Because when we try to remember a list, a poem, a speech, or even a phone number, a different part of our brain is being activated than the "cookie-smelling, music-hearing" part.

When we try to learn words and numbers on their own, the more recently evolved and developed frontal lobes—where language comprehension and critical thinking occur—are being accessed. This is the part of the brain that we use in most classrooms, the part that is reading these words right now . . . the same part of your brain that is considering and analyzing what I've said (as well as perhaps trying to memorize as many states as possible in alphabetical order without music!).

This part of our minds is incredibly useful. It gives us the ability to think critically and use language, to reason, to judge, and to discern. It is the part that allows us to memorize and hold information in short-term storage.

Helpful and necessary as it is, our short-term memory has a relatively limited capacity. Phone numbers are seven digits for a reason, the same reason that self-help and business books rarely tout more than seven tips, habits, or tools for improvement. Our minds, in this way, have difficulty processing and holding greater amounts of information.

When we blend content with sounds, smells, or emotion, however—or with physical experience, as we discussed in *The Art of Singing* when it comes to vocal learning—we are granted access to a very different process of memory acquisition. Bypassing our intellects and conscious thinking entirely, these sensory experiences trigger our long-term memory stores, housed in the oldest, pre-language parts of our brains: the basal ganglia and amygdala.

Why are the two so different? Because short-term and long-term memory came into being at two different times, under two different sets of circumstances, and to serve two different purposes.

The Evolution of Memory

Many people wouldn't be surprised that a dog abused long ago over a period of time will still flinch when you reach to pet him; we humans also have this type of enduring conditioned response. That said, isn't it interesting that the same dog will immediately "forget" a verbal rebuke or a fight with another dog, bounding gleefully back to either scene moments later as if nothing happened?

Ted Kerasote illustrates this phenomenon in his wonderful book *Merle's Door*. His long-time canine friend never got over his aversion to shotguns, with which he'd had terrible experiences as a puppy. Yet of emotions, Kerasote says this of Merle:

> "He was one of the best examples of how to deal with disappointment and ride through anger, for it was apparent that he had no interest in his emotions becoming him. He clung to them the way our mountains clung to their weather, then let them roll over him and fade away."[10]

I'm not comparing us to dogs, much as I adore them. Rather, I'm trying to highlight that our cognitive processing and short-term memory capabilities are, evolutionarily speaking, more recent and human-specific developments.[11] Babies behave in a similar fashion to dogs in the first months of their lives before these aspects of the brain more fully form; in hysterics one moment and gurgling the next, they too have the ability to completely get over what has happened (whereas adults tend to hold on to events through intellectual judgments).

Language and Memory

For centuries, we adult humans were the same way. Our ancestors didn't utilize what we know today to be short-term memory storage because, for starters, they didn't have anything to store the information *in*. Before the existence of complex language, the corresponding parts of the brain hadn't fully developed.

This is in part because early humans didn't have the need to store information in this manner. Life occurred in the moment (as it does with dogs and babies) and all knowledge was directly related to survival. It was only later, when humans were reliably able to access resources and ensure their physical existence, that the frontal lobes began to more fully develop, with complex language, active reflection, and higher reasoning becoming possible as a result.

Until that time, everything required for the perpetuation of a community and culture had to be transmitted in a manner that ensured its place in long-term, emotionalized memory. And given the unique capability of melody and music to capture and store information, all communication was therefore "sung."

The Role of the Voice

While today, the idea of musical communication might seem strange, it wasn't for our ancestors. There wasn't a thought as to whether someone was "singing" or "speaking," as they hadn't yet been experienced or defined as separate. The two, for all intents and purposes, were collapsed, as they are with children today. The focus was on conveying meaning, strengthening a bond, or initiating action, with vocalizations taking the form of whatever blend of tone, melody, and rhythm was required to do so.

For thousands of years, it was a biological imperative to be musical. Not sometimes, not occasionally . . . all of the time. For communication and for celebration; in warring, in warning, and in wooing. For creating the future and for honoring the past; when bringing new life into the world, and when releasing those from it whose time had come.

For everything under the sun, moon, and stars—and in acknowledgment of their mysteries—we sang.

CHAPTER THREE

The Rise of the New Voice

Obviously, a lot has changed since then. Let's take a look at the three largest shifts in communication since the time of our ancestors and what they mean for us today as singers and performers.

Musicality: From Song to Speech

Language, Content, and Memory

Today, it is no longer a biological imperative to sing. As we explored in the last chapter, language and our increased physical proximity have diminished our need for sharp vocal distinctions and volume. Words rather than a broad use of melody and percussion communicate what we want to express more than sufficiently.

The content of what we want to express has changed as well. Now that we are secure in our physical survival, our focus today is on literature, philosophy, and art . . . on math, science, and politics, to name a few. These and other popular topics are important and nourishing in many ways, yet they feed our intellects more than help our biological perpetuation. As such, they're not required to be pulled into our emotionalized, long-term memory stores through musical communication.

We have also become less reliant upon memory. Writing and technology have made it possible to store both survival-related and cursory information externally, taking away the demand for constant engagement with both our long- and short-term recall abilities. The minute I put something on my calendar or to-do list, I forget it . . . because I can.

Physical Conditioning

Because of our reliance upon language, the non-survival-related content of our modern conversations, and our technological substitutes for memory (and vocal projection), the demand for the fullness of our musically expressive range in daily communication has virtually disappeared. And as that need has disappeared, so too has the physical conditioning that once supported it.

We are left using a new kind of voice, which is very different from the one used by our ancestors. It is a voice with less volume, emotion, and energy. One with less range and power. And while it is effective in our modern-day communications, it has left the majority of us out of touch and practice with our musical voice.

Meaning: From Communal to Individual Experience

Personal, Dually Relevant, and Relational Communication

The spirit and essence of our conversations have altered as well. For our ancestors, communication was personal. It was sent directly from someone to someone. Biology prevented any other possibility. Whether individually or in a group, people knew with whom they were speaking. Even with an outsider, there was always a sure sense of who would be receiving the message.

They also knew why something was being communicated. The survival of a community relied upon the vocal transfer of knowledge and information, meaning that all communication was as important to the deliverer as to the receiver. Every participant had a vested interest in what was being said and listened for it.

Lastly, communication did more than deliver information from one person or group to another. It was intended to bond or bind them together.[1] Power existed as strength in numbers and solidarity. Communication and rituals of every kind were an opportunity to reinforce each person's role and purpose in the community, as well as to better know one another, and to be known.

The Deterioration of Connection

Today, this is no longer the case. We're vastly less communal and connected, in spite of our closer physical proximity. We no longer need to relate to and rely upon each other in order to survive, and therefore we don't. We live in towns, communities, and even buildings without knowing many of our neighbors. We go to the grocery store, not only unaware of where our food comes from, but disconnected from the necessity— and the opportunity—of growing and harvesting it together. All we need is a credit card and everything necessary to survive, largely on our own, is available to us.

Without the mutual and interdependent purpose of survival, we've not only become less connected to one another, we've also begun to develop the cultural habit of avoidance. In the elevator, walking in town, standing in line for a movie and even sitting in the very next seat, we avoid engaging with and sometimes even looking at one another. I often marvel when I'm out for dinner that it seems we've all chosen to leave our houses for a bit of social interaction, only to virtually ignore the people around us. Yet if it was just the food we wanted, we could have called for delivery or taken our order home!

The Decline of Listening

> "Most people do not listen with the intent to understand; they listen with the intent to reply."
>
> —Stephen R. Covey, Author, *The 7 Habits of Highly Effective People*[2]

This conditioning has not only changed *what* we talk about, but *how* we talk and listen as well. Because we no longer need precision in our conversations, they often become exercises in getting a point across and trying to be right rather than listening to and connecting with others. Opportunities for intimacy are no longer a given; for many they are few and far between and sometimes even surprising.

We even use our speech to avoid real communication, asking and answering questions in a way that deflects rather than engages connection with others. As we talked about in *The Art of Singing*, how often do we say hello and ask how people are doing with any real intention or interest in hearing what they have to say in response?

As a result, while we obviously still speak to one another, we're not always *communicating*. Compared to our ancestors, our conversations are vastly more impersonal and irrelevant. We've become disconnected even in our connection, often finding ourselves removed from those we are close to. Surrounded by people, many of us are very much alone.

Manageability: From Confidence to Caution

Distance and Proximity

Finally, since the time of our ancestors, we have lost the ability to manage our conversations. Thanks to technology, we're often not in the same room as those with whom we're speaking. Sometimes, we've never met or don't know them at all. While the content of our conversations may move us forward, on the phone or over e-mail we're unable to fully process people, leaving us separated in more ways than one.

Interestingly, the same is now true in many of our in-person interactions as well. The body gives off chemicals that help us get to know one another. The Latin introduction of kissing on each cheek and the Arab and African embrace stem from our desire and even need to take in and process those with whom we're engaging.[3]

Important as these chemicals are, we've culturally developed the habit of resisting our instinctive desire to get close to one another. While people still shake hands and sometimes hug as a greeting here in the States, our actions tend to be much more cursory. With our innate ability to discern authenticity "turned off," our intellects are left with the responsibility of processing what information is available and trying to create the missing details.

Unfortunately, the result is our responding more to our own assumptions and judgments about other people, rather than their real essence and intentions. Which is why, even after months of spending time with someone, a relationship may still feel hollow or unsatisfying. We may have grown familiar thanks to intellectual effort, but still may not really know each other.

Authenticity

This is certainly true as well when it comes to the media, where it is an even greater challenge to discern authenticity. In today's digital world, only our eyes and ears are the test . . . but a test of what? What is being delivered in songs, movies, and politics is scripted and rehearsed long before it is actually shared. Too often, effectiveness as a communicator is about how you look and sound rather than by how much of the truth you're telling. Appearance, persuasion, and selling, rather than meaning, are the benchmarks of modern broadcasting, often resulting in a hollowness in what is being delivered, as well as in the delivery itself.

Control

Finally, we've also lost control of our conversations. Thanks to technology, we no longer know where what we say or write is going or what it will be used for. We don't know who will hear it, how they'll use it, or what they'll make it mean. We're unable to ensure that we're delivering our words, voices, and selves to people who will continue to share our messages in alignment with our intended purposes.

I'm reminded of the Native Americans who famously resisted being photographed for fear of their souls being captured. While this notion might seem odd to many of us, it makes sense from the worldview of personal, dually relevant, and relational communication. There was always a sense of how and how far our ancestors' words and "selves" would travel. There was a sure knowledge of to whom a message was being delivered. Even between generations, there was a direct and meaningful connection—a thread of purpose—that ran from the speaker down through the lines of time and history.[4]

To the Native Americans, people unknown and unassociated with their values and community wanting to "take" them somewhere they'd never been was unfathomable. Yet this is precisely what we do today. We dash off e-mails, leave voice messages, and post pictures and videos on the Internet without much thought or understanding as to where they eventually might go, who will see them, and what in time they could be used for.

And of course, we love this modern way of interacting! I've gotten to know many of you through e-mail and Facebook, and am incredibly grateful for our conversations and relationships. I wouldn't trade them for the world.

In spite of the benefits, however, the fundamental unmanageability of our digital communications has had an impact on our ability to connect with complete trust, confidence, and ease . . . whether we realize it or not. A type of hesitance and even wariness has set in, not only in our online interactions, but also in our sense of self as we extend in every way into the world.

The Three Changes

On the surface, these descriptions sound pretty bleak. It sounds like I'm saying that we are a bunch of insecure people who don't care about and can't connect with our families, friends, neighbors, and communities.

Believe me, that's not what I'm saying. Most of us, myself included, have great relationships with the people in our lives—relationships that we value and cherish.

Yet from the perspective of history, all of our interactions have altered dramatically, and not necessarily for the better. Regardless of how vulnerable and open we personally might be, collectively, the voice of our ancestors is no longer an instrument we use. It is no longer a communion we share. And it is no longer an expression we trust.

CHAPTER FOUR

The Birth of Performance and Performance Anxiety

In the place of our ancestral voice, three new distinctions have emerged that encompass our modern voice, including how we use, relate to, and experience it:

- By moving from song to speech, what we now call singing has come into being.
- Shifting from a communal to an individual experience has led to the rise of performance as a cultural construct.
- Finally, our transition from confidence to caution in our relationships has laid the foundation for what we experience today as performance anxiety.

Singing

"When all of these people tell me they can't 'find' their voice, they are assuming they don't have one . . . It's easier to believe that the voice is not there than to recognize that we are actually standing in its way."

—Silvia Nakkach, Author, *Free Your Voice*[1]

Unlike many aspects of evolution, where one thing eventually replaces another, our musical voice hasn't gone away. Nor has our desire to use it. Just as our bodies crave the stimulation of an intense run or the release of a deep massage, singing activates the breath and body in a way that promotes longevity and well-being. For spirituality, self-expression, and health, we still yearn to use our voices beyond what speech allows for.

In spite of this desire, it is not one that everyone fulfills. Once the singsong voice of early childhood is fully replaced by speech, its musical aspects are not used again unless consciously chosen. And in our culture, particularly as we get older, that choice tends to be made less and less.

Unfortunately, more than the amount of time spent singing has changed. The belief has also emerged that it and speaking are completely different entities.

This isn't the case. Anatomically identical and equally accessible, we merely perceive them as separate. First evolutionarily, then culturally, a sharp divide has formed between the voice and The Voice, with singing as a result becoming experientially what it has been predicted to be . . . difficult, or at the very least, much harder than speaking.

Because singing is no longer experienced by many people as an effortless process, thanks to incorrect beliefs and a lack of regular engagement, it is now seen as something challenging to learn and, as a result, something that must be taught. In universities, conservatories, and private studios around the world, education has therefore been devised to bridge a gap that we ourselves have created.

> "We can no more explain who we are and how we act in terms of our brain activity than we would explain a dance in terms of a muscle."
> —Alva Noë, Professor of Philosophy at the University of California, Berkeley[2]

In spite of people's best efforts, however, this gap is not always bridged. Rarely do we recover the automatic vocal relationship from our childhoods or unmask the full, musical voice our ancestors once knew. Relying on the intellect to guide us in unlocking what appear to be the mysteries of the singing voice, we instead try to isolate and interact with interdependent physical systems. We attempt to cerebrally direct primarily automatic mechanisms, rather than to first allow and observe their engagement.[3]

Said another way, we try to arrange individual pieces of an unknown puzzle, rather than first looking for the holistic view.

Understandably, many people have trouble with this approach. Yet these results are not seen as victories or failures of the teaching methodology. Instead, they are seen as confirmation of three popular though inaccurate current cultural beliefs:

- Singing is difficult.
- Singing requires an uncommon talent.
- Singing and the few who do it well are inherently special.

Performing

For many people, these incorrect beliefs also apply to performing, which diminishes the experience of both and makes it easy to overlook the differences between them. Singing is a physical act; performing is a gesture of expression. Singing involves a specific vocal engagement; performing encompasses a variety of activities, including dancing, acting, speaking, and even silence. Singing may be done alone or with people; performing requires the presence of at least one other person.

Performance as Presentation

The last sentence often makes people pause. Is it not possible to perform when we are alone? No, when we are by ourselves, we call the same activities singing, dancing, and speaking. We may even call engaging in them practicing. But when we are alone, we don't say that we are performing. To sing is to sing. To perform is to sing *in front of.*

A performance is any type of planned or improvised *public* demonstration. Whether televised, recorded, or live, whether in an arena or in a friend's living room, it is an act of sharing before witnesses. And this presentational notion of performance has existed for centuries, originally in the form of rituals and rites and more recently in shows, concerts, and other modern mediums with which we are all familiar.

Performance as Cultural Experience

Right now, we are going to set aside this presentational aspect of performance and focus on a new experience of performing that has recently come into being, as well as how and why it emerged. For just as the development of language led to the creation of "singing" as both a term and an experience, shifts in our communication have led to the emergence of an entirely new type of "performance" in our culture as well.

These shifts aren't voice related, per se. Rather, they stem from the decreased meaning of our conversations and the reduced amount of connectedness we have in those interactions. As we moved away from personal, relational, and dually relevant communication, touching, talking, and even being with one another began to be experienced very differently. No longer commonplace, they became less usual and eventually, less comfortable.

That's not to say that meaning, comfort, and connectedness went away altogether. As we discussed in the last chapter, with friends we can joke and feel open and relaxed; with loved ones we can talk about our day with comfort and ease. There is no performance going on here. We are not in front of our family and friends. We are *with them*.

Yet when asked to share the same retelling of your day or a joke with a group of people you don't know—and even some you do—the experience often alters dramatically. We might say the same words and deliver the same punch lines, but in the absence of intimacy, internal caution becomes externalized, slightly or greatly changing our delivery.

No longer communicating as it was defined and experienced for centuries, we move into something more along the lines of a performance, given the divide that now exists between us and other people, and our uncertainty of how to bridge it on command.

The word *performance* literally means: "to carry out, to execute, to go through."[4] And while it certainly applies to the presentational aspects of performance we talked about a moment ago—we carry out theatrical plays, execute dance routines, and go through musical sets—doesn't it also apply to many of our personal interactions today as well? In our schools, communities, and workplaces, how often do we find ourselves "going through" the motions with the people in our lives, rather than actually communicating with them? It makes you wonder, in certain instances, why we bother.

The reason is simple. Just as the desire to sing remains, we also still long to connect deeply with one another. No matter how out of practice we may be or how unnecessary (for survival) it may seem, we want to be close to other people, even if we are no longer as adept at managing togetherness. It remains an engrained part of our nature as social beings, even if it is no longer a requirement of our culture.

Therefore, just as we've developed training to compensate for the decreased use of our musical voice, we've created opportunities to learn how to reconnect with one another. We take classes on "self-expression," "public speaking," and "persuasion." We go to workshops on the arts of "vulnerability" and "intimacy."

Just as a "singer" now "performs" upon a "stage" before an "audience."

There is nothing wrong with any of these terms. They merely point to new, modern-day experiences that are increasingly removed from what our ancestors called the same practices—even those where individuals danced, spoke, and sang in front of others: *being together*.

There were no separate terms for sharing, connecting, and expressing for our ancestors, because there was rarely a time when they weren't accomplishing all three. Even in ceremonies before the entire community, they were with rather than in front of others. There wasn't a need to close an intimacy gap between people, as there was never one to begin with.

In this sense, there is no performing in reality . . . only our perception makes it so. Today, as we move from what can only be called a semi-engaged state to one of direct interaction, we enter unfamiliar and often uncomfortable territory, resulting in our feeling as though we are indeed performing, rather than being with other people.

∾

A note: these descriptions of singing and performing are obviously only the beginning of their respective conversations. In the presentational sense, masterful singing involves more than allowing for a reflexive engagement, just as performing requires more than gaining comfort being with people.

Remember that here, we're looking at singing and performing from a cultural perspective. We're establishing the starting point of how they came into being, so that we can understand what so many singers and performers are dealing with when they approach the stage and studio. Rest assured, we'll be talking more about the presentational aspects of both later in the book.

Performance Anxiety

> "The meaning of a word isn't found ultimately in a dictionary, but rather, in its usage."
> —Mark L. Ward Jr. [5]

While singing and performing appear similar and are often collapsed, performing and performance anxiety are so linked in both theory and practice that it can be tough to tease them apart.

That said, the two are indeed distinct. As we just discussed, performance is an act of expression or engagement. It simply means to sing (or speak, or dance) in front of others—that there is a presentation occurring, given either by the reality or the perception of distance between people.

There is no inherent anxiety in performance, no matter how nervous you may get. The adverse emotional and physical experience so common in performance today is wholly contained within the notion of *performance anxiety* itself—an anxiety that far surpasses the social discomfort that so often accompanies being with others.

To bring home how separate the two actually are, consider that it's not only possible to perform without anxiety; it's also common to have performance anxiety in the absence of both performing and other people.

We've already discussed how for our ancestors, "performing" didn't necessarily evoke nervousness, as their experience was one of being together. We may have comparable experiences when sharing with our families or telling a joke to a group of friends.

Similarly, a speaker today might be so at ease with others and herself—so willing to be open, vulnerable, and sincere—that she doesn't get nervous when giving even a very public speech. The same is true for many musicians I know and have worked with, who only experience a sense of having fun and "being in the zone" when they're onstage.

For these men and women, the negative experience of anxiety is so absent that they often go a step further in their description of the situation, insisting that "performance" is absent as well. Our speaker might say that she is simply "speaking"; the musicians I know, that they are just "playing."

In all areas of life, we reach for language to try to describe our experiences. Sometimes it does a good job, sometimes it doesn't.[6] Given that anxiety is so often implied in performance, it makes sense that these fear-free men and women might throw both words away in their effort to disassociate themselves from an experience they don't have.

In terms of performance anxiety existing in the absence of a presentation, see if you can't locate a personal example. I certainly can; just thinking of an upcoming singing engagement, I've felt anxiety and nervousness. Sitting alone in my office, my face has flushed and my heart raced at the thought of giving a lecture or workshop even months away.

The Physiology of Performance Anxiety

"Fear is a negative emotion unless you are facing an actual threat."
—Deepak Chopra[7]

What are these symptoms all about? Known as the *fight-or-flight response*, they signal that our bodies are preparing us for a real or perceived danger. Cortisol and adrenaline flow into the bloodstream, enhancing our mental acuity and physical readiness for whatever situation we may be facing, on or off the stage. And along with them come the butterflies, sweaty palms, and hand shakes with which we are all familiar.

Interestingly, the same hormones and sensations are also present when we're excited.[8] Think about it . . . on an amazing first date, aren't you also nervous? Your mouth goes dry and your palms start to sweat, just as they do when you're surprised by friends, wrapped up in a game or concert you love, or thrill seeking.

If the physiology of fear and excitement is so similar, why don't we feel the same sense of joy and adventure when we're performing, instead of the panic, nerves, and all-around awfulness so many of us deal with?

To a large extent, the answer is that we have collectively decided not to. Over time, two very powerful beliefs have emerged and adversely altered the way we relate to and experience performing. And a direct byproduct of these two beliefs is the terrible anxiety most of us grapple with.

Type One: Significance-Related Performance Anxiety

The first type of performance anxiety is an extension of the social discomfort that arises when we attempt to connect with people beyond a cursory engagement; the discomfort that comes from standing before, rather than with, a group of people.

We have all experienced this type of performance anxiety to some degree, even if we've never sung a note in our lives. It's been said that the fear of public speaking is greater than the fear of death for a reason: no matter who we are or what we do, getting in front of people when we're not comfortable being with them can be unsettling and even alarming.

Discomfort by itself isn't the problem, however. Pulled muscles and awkward situations are uncomfortable. Yet no matter where they fall on the continuum of unsettling to distressing, they don't rival the fear of dying!

What turns discomfort into something more serious—what elevates it to the level of anxiety and even panic—is the significance, or meaning, that we add to it. And as a result, the way we think about and relate to it.

When we're asked to speak before a group, the majority of us don't think: "Wow, I don't have much experience being vulnerable and intimate with people. Perhaps I should look into why this is and consider making some changes." That might be an appropriate reaction to socially conditioned discomfort.

Instead, a more common response to speaking or singing in public runs along the following lines, generally accompanied by a heavy dose of fear: "Oh my goodness . . . I can't handle this. I can't do it. What will people think of me? I'm going to fall apart. I can't take this . . . my heart is racing . . . I won't do it! I would rather *die* than get on that stage!"

The intensity is palpable. Just reading the words, some of you may even be transported back to your own experiences of panic and terror.

In these situations, we're clearly grappling with something far more substantial than the discomfort that comes from not being connected with other people. And what that is—the significance we've added to performance—is a concern for our personal well-being. Put simply, we've come to believe that situations involving getting up in front of other people are unsafe, and that we are unsafe in them.

How did we come to attach the idea of safety to performance?

I have a friend who once said that you should never believe anything your mind tells you between the hours of two and five in the morning. He has a point; lying in the dark in the middle of the night, it is amazing what real-seeming and tragic tales our minds can come up with . . . tales that dissolve into ludicrousness with the rising of the sun.

The same is true of significance-related performance anxiety. Once we have spoken or sung, it is incredible to reflect upon how terrified, panicked—and even ill!—we became in the face of what turned out to be a harmless experience.

As physically safe as giving a speech or a concert may be, our fears and late-night thinking do have a basis in reality—a reality that extends back to the time of our ancestors. While today we no longer worry about our actual survival as they had to, we *are* concerned with safeguarding our intellectual and emotional well-being, which together form the essence of who most of us know ourselves to be.

Above and beyond our physical bodies, we're therefore determined to protect this sense of self at all costs. Which means that when we're put on the spot or into the spotlight—or even when we imagine these scenarios—our egos are doing nothing short of fighting for survival.

And what are they fighting against? Judgment.

Judgment's Role in Performance Anxiety

A conception of self—a notion of "me"—has always existed. Even in collective, pre-language communities, there has always been some distinction between the observer and the observed.

Yet the distinction wasn't originally negative. We were separate, but still the same. The development of language and our brain's evolving method of categorization were gifts that allowed people to more rapidly perceive what made them unique, as well as to name those differences.

Over time, however, as our interdependence and connection have slipped away and our cultural avoidance has increased, our ability to categorize has taken on a pejorative flavor. In a mode of constant self-protection, it has transformed into an ongoing judgment of others and by extension, of ourselves—a judgment that is amplified when it is our turn to speak or sing.

We may not physically banish outsiders, as some of our ancestors did, but we do intellectually and emotionally shun and ostracize all the time—the effects of which are often just as painful and crippling as if we were left out in the cold to starve to death.

When we stand before a group, we're not worried that someone is going to actually exile or shoot us. But we may as well be. We are just as fearful of the weapon of judgment being turned upon us and cower in its line of fire.

Dealing with Judgment-Related Performance Anxiety

While we logically know that fear and judgment won't cause us physical harm, awareness has little success in changing a survival-related viewpoint. Instead, the solution is to replace our fearful and unhealthy reactions with more empowering ones. And when it comes to singing, speaking, or performing of any kind, there's only one way to go about this: *lots of public practice.*

I always share this advice with my clients who are nervous about their upcoming performances. And so many of them are . . . they love to sing, but are often horrified about the actual experience of doing so in public. Their minds run amok with the countless disasters that might befall them, including of course the "deathly" possibility of making mistakes, being judged, and found unworthy.

What's interesting is how many attempt to lessen their terror by spending endless amounts of time trying to think about their performances, themselves, and the relationship between the two differently. When in fact, what's needed is simply for them to get out there and *sing.*

If you have a show in a month, ruminating and stressing about it from now until then will not help you. Singing in front of an audience three times a week for the next four weeks, on the other hand, will. If you need to read a poem at a friend's wedding or to give a presentation at work, ask friends, family, and colleagues if you can run through it for them every chance you get.

Trust me, the fear this suggestion might bring up and the anxiety you'll feel the first couple of times you get in front of a group will diminish with each experience. Will you make mistakes? Of course . . . and you'll realize that you can survive them. Will people judge you? Absolutely . . . and you'll live to tell the tale.

Singing in your shower, practice room, or during voice lessons won't help when it comes to dealing with fears of failure and judgment. Singing in public will. It is simply the only way to get out of your head and into the reality of being in front of—and eventually with—other people. Mistakes are inevitable and everyone has an opinion. In all areas of your life, it's up to you to decide whether or not you'll allow either to stop you from sharing yourself and enjoying the experience.

TECHNOLOGY'S ROLE IN PERFORMANCE ANXIETY

Communication-related technology has also had a hand in the rise of this first type of performance anxiety. No matter how well we've learned to accommodate its presence and the pace at which it has come about, we also operate on another level that is virtually impossible for us manage or control. And that is the level of our older, mammalian brain.

When someone puts a microphone or camera in front of us and asks us to speak or sing, regardless of how we might feel about the experience, we often panic because we can't viscerally manage this form of communication. Electronic amplification and digital distribution do not exist in nature and therefore don't make sense to the older aspects of our minds. If you doubt this, notice how often young children clam up when a phone or video monitor is placed in front of them.

We can't wrap our heads around how our voices and we can be shared with an infinite number of people, including those not in our presence. To say nothing of the reactions that we can't take in, process, and respond to.

This outpouring of the self without feedback not only leaves us feeling wary and insecure, it also causes anxiety on a more animalistic level. In these situations, it doesn't matter how adept we are at being with others or how much we've practiced. There are only so many people at a time we can fully sense, be aware of, and connect with.

Dealing with Technology in Performance Anxiety

Thankfully, we're not all doomed to a life of stress if we want to share our talents with more than a few people at a time. As with the speaker and musicians I mentioned a few pages ago, there are ways to get around the anxiety-provoking experience of being in front of large and widespread groups.

One approach has to do with developing a greater amount of intimacy with your audience by shifting the way you perceive the people in it. Rather than seeing them as countless, nameless, and unknown entities whose judgment you fear, shift your intention to sharing yourself openly and getting to know them. Preoccupy yourself with wondering about who the people are sitting there before you, not only collectively, but also individually. What do they want and need? What are they looking for in their lives? Imagine that they have come to your home to share a meal and discuss their concerns, their ideas, and their dreams. How would you reach out to them? How would you help?

Those who come to experience your sharing onstage are no different. While they are there to listen to you, they are in fact asking to be heard. They are waiting to be touched and to feel inspired. They are longing to experience something in your voice and expression that will open them up further to themselves.

You might be the one onstage, but it's not all about you . . . or it doesn't have to be. And if you can make this shift—from performance being a one-way offering of yourself, to it being an invitation to intimacy, participation with, and even a service to others—the fear of judgment and grip of performance anxiety begin to unravel and fade.

Another technique is to mentally reframe the audience to a size that is comfortable for you to manage. For example, by focusing on one or a few members of the group as if they were the only ones present, or alternatively, seeing the whole audience or the camera as a single entity or spirit with whom you can connect, many are able to convince the mind to relax its anxiety about the unmanageability of the actual numbers.

I've used both of these approaches when singing in arenas, on TV, and even in intimate groups. Having them become your automatic default way of thinking takes a good deal of practice and patience, just like meditation or any other mind-body discipline. Yet they are well worth it. Not only do they help to dissipate anxiety, they also allow you recapture the joy of sharing yourself and your voice with others.

A final approach is to learn how to ignore your audience; to be so involved in your singing, playing, and performing that you are for the most part unaware of those around you. While this technique works for some people—and certain artists naturally go this deeply into the zone—I don't recommend practicing it as a tool, as any number of things can snap you out of your cocoon and back into reality unprepared. Many people I've worked with have found themselves in such moments, standing onstage like a deer in the headlights with no idea of what to do or where to go.

Type Two: Value-Related Performance Anxiety

> "When we were children, what did we do? We played with our voices as if they were shiny new toys with unlimited potential for joy and expression. Nothing stood in our way."
>
> —Silvia Nakkach, Author, *Free Your Voice*[9]

The second type of performance anxiety is notorious in the performing realm and in my experience is more challenging to deal with. For these individuals, anxiety not only stems from the decline of connection and the rise of technology; it also comes from their personal value and self-worth being wrapped up with their creativity.

With significance-related performance anxiety, something is wrong with the situation and their ability to handle it. With value-related performance anxiety, something is wrong *with them*.

We now come full circle to the "specialness" we talked about at the beginning of this chapter, as well as to a better understanding of how the concepts of singing, performing, and performance anxiety have become so experientially intertwined.

In *The Art of Singing*, we spend a good deal of time talking about the personal and psychological challenges that often accompany singing, many of which begin at a very young age. And while every person's experience is different, the stories I've heard over the years from hundreds of singers grappling with this type of anxiety are largely the same.

As we've discussed, there is no divide between singing and speaking when we're young. The two are essentially blended. Everything is mixed up in an undefined, unnamed, happy hybrid of babbling and sound making.

The amazement that meets our first steps and words are showered upon our first melodies and songs as well. Yet unlike the accolades that fade once walking and talking are mastered, praise for singing often continues. And increases.

Rather quickly, a different kind and amount of attention is given to these children when they sing. What they started out doing for fun, or just doing, is suddenly being rewarded with praise, admiration, and even affection. Their singing seems to be something pretty special, and hey . . . so do they!

And so they keep singing.

Some children go through this phase with little consequence. They either don't notice or casually appreciate that their singing brings joy to and attention from those around them. As a result, it remains something fun to do; their personal value doesn't get attached to it.

Others, however, have a very different experience, particularly in situations where attention, praise, or rewards are or are perceived to be lacking. For these children, as well as some in entirely stable environments, an uncertain or developing sense of self not only notices, but also starts to believe certain things as the people around them begin to recognize their voices, including:

People become happy when I sing.
People stop fighting when I sing.
People pay attention to me.
People leave me alone.
People treat me well.
People think I'm talented.
People think I'm special.

These messages and interpretations tend to increase once these children enter school, where the notion that they are special *because* of their voices is not only implied, but is often implicitly stated.[10] While others struggle with fitting in and feeling good about themselves, our young singers are met with praise, purpose, and sometimes popularity thanks to their voices. This "advantage" stays with them into their teens and twenties, and—unless another skill, talent, or more powerful sense of self is developed and leaned upon—follows them as they enter adulthood, along with thoughts such as:

Singing is something that will make me succeed.
Singing is something that will get me out of here.
Singing will make me famous.
Singing will make me rich.
Singing will set me apart
Singing is something that will prove how great I am.

The longing to distinguish ourselves is powerful and is a part of our social, academic, and professional cultures. It's not unique to singing; whether we're smart, athletic, funny, or attractive, the desire to claim and exploit our strengths is common to all of us.

And there's nothing wrong with having talent, great grades, a sense of humor, or good looks.

The problem is that we are often encouraged to believe that we are special *because* of these gifts, rather than that we—connected with, equal to, and as inherently worthy as everyone else—happen to have certain gifts that are seen as culturally special.

For many people, and certainly for the singers we are discussing, this little distinction creates a huge shift of experience. Instead of hearing "people like that I sing," the message heard, regardless of what is actually said, is that "people like me *because* I sing." The voice becomes a main aspect, if not a leader, of the forward face these singers present to the world. Who are they without it? They don't know. And they're terrified to find out.

As a result, every time these young men and women sing, every time they get onstage, they not only have to deal with bridging the interpersonal divides in our culture and the discomfort stemming from advances in technology. They also have to deal with their own personal sense of value and worth being on the line. In every performance and even in the anticipation of them, they are doing nothing less than fighting for their lives.

It's therefore not surprising that much of the joy that drew these men and women to singing in the first place is now gone. How could it be otherwise, when their self-confidence and esteem are always at risk?

Consider most singers you know. Consider yourself. How many of them—how many of you—eagerly respond when asked to sing on the spot, whether at a party or in someone's home? While some are happy to oblige, in my experience, many more are not. And the decline isn't passive. If only internally, these situations are often heavy and fraught with anxiety and angst. So much so that the only way some are able to break free is to abandon public singing altogether.

This unhealthy relationship with the voice gets so ingrained over the years that logic and practice are unable to dismantle it. Explanations that the person rather than the voice is what is truly precious do little good. The seed was planted by culture, watered by family and friends, nurtured by school and training, and pruned by the shears of competition, insecurity, and the desire to be unique, successful, and special.

The result? The belief that the voice is what grants personal value growing out of control, choking everything else in its path.

This is what a good number of singers walk into the recording studio and onto the stage with. *This* is what they bring with them into their careers and relationships; what they carry with them through life. So much drama hindering a beautiful and natural form of expression; so much stress around what—while meaningful—is an inherently normal, insignificant act.

Who knows for certain why some people plow into this type of relationship with singing and how others manage to avoid it. As in all things, many factors influence outcome. That said, there came a moment when each of us made a decision about how we would interact with music and singing in the world, regardless of how we first personally experienced them. Not all of us chose wisely, or even consciously. But at some point, those of us who sing either rejected or agreed to this all too common cultural view of personal performance worth . . . a decision that has profoundly shaped our careers and lives, as well as our ability to enjoy them.

A New Beginning

"Misery seems to be downhill; ecstasy seems to be uphill. Ecstasy looks very difficult to reach—but it is not so. Society has done a great job. It has made miserable creatures out of ecstatic creators. Every child is born ecstatic."

—Osho, Mystic and Spiritual Teacher[11]

Right now, do me a favor. It doesn't matter whether you're a singer or an engineer, whether you're a teacher or a student . . . whether you're a consummate performer or someone who has never stepped foot on a stage or sung a note in your life.

Think back to what it must have been like for our ancestors, to be a part of something larger than yourself. To have a voice, and the deep, self-assured knowledge and confidence that it is your right to use it. Effortlessly, powerfully, joyfully, and musically.

Place your hand on your belly and feel the breath coming into your body. Then feel it going out. Take a moment and connect back in time with all those who have come before you, as well as those who will come after.

Then, doing everything you can to set aside any resistance you might feel, open your mouth and allow yourself to say and then sing something. Feel the voice inside of you reverberating. Your voice. The vehicle of your spirit; the communicator of your heart.

When you allow yourself the opportunity to connect with what your body is meant to do—what it has always been meant to do—you also connect with the essence of *who you really are*. And when you give yourself permission to use your voice, you return to the state of peace, confidence, and love that allows you to open up and share yourself—your real self—with others and the world around you.

≈

While it's normal to experience some fear and anxiety when we perform, the reasons we remain tethered and shackled to the most intense and painful versions of these feelings often have more to do with how we feel about ourselves than we do about our voices and performance. Righteousness and arrogance are the opposing magnets that keep peace and performing apart. Wanting to be better than others, to be perfect, to look good, and to justify ourselves . . . every day, we trade these and other ego-based ambitions for the freedom and joy of being self-expressed, both personally and vocally.

Thankfully, when we use our voices as our ancestors did, we enter into a state of grace that snaps us out of this zero sum game. In this space, the cheap prizes we've been holding on to become clear, as does the incredible future that is available to us when we choose our voices over our fear. When we choose ourselves over our pride. When we choose acceptance. When we choose love.

This future has always been there waiting for us. It is waiting there right now for you.

PART TWO

Enter the Cast

CHAPTER FIVE

Singers, Producers, and Engineers

Understanding where we've come from is the key to getting where we want to go successfully. Equally important is taking stock of where we are now, as we are as much the product of our present-day culture as we are unique individuals.

Having read Part One, you no longer have only your own experiences as a reference. You also have a better sense of why you and others grapple with technology and performing today, as well as an understanding of how many of those common experiences came into being.

The way we perceive and interact with others is equally influenced by our past experiences, as well as our current cultural agreements and personal viewpoints. As such, our impressions of other people and the dynamics we have with them aren't necessarily accurate or inevitable. They're subjective and influenced by a variety of factors, as are singing, performing, and performance anxiety.

Knowing this gives us the perspective required to see ourselves, others, and the world more objectively. In turn, it allows us to shape our relationships and circumstances to work in our favor; to recognize and set aside what hasn't been working, so that we can create what does.

We spent the first part of the book doing just that with technology, the voice, and performing. Now, let's turn our attention to the relationships between singers, producers, and engineers.

Are You Ready?

Unlike the last section where we were observers of the past, we're now going to take a front row seat and watch ourselves on the big screen.

As I mentioned in the introduction, I'm not attempting to define performers or technicians. Every one of us is an individual and I've known as many singers who break the "singer mold" as I have engineers and producers who do the same. Many work beautifully together, enjoy the process, and in no way embody the issues we are about to explore.

We're also not going down this road to blame anyone, to make anyone wrong, or to imply that one person or group is better than another. We all have strengths and weakness, both professionally and personally. No one group or profession has a lock on being tapped into the former more than the latter.

What we are going to do is discuss some tendencies, which often result in common yet ineffective interactions onstage and in the studio. By highlighting and understanding these dynamics, we have a shot at transforming them—a process we can accomplish only once we have a sense of where these issues come from as well as why they tend to play out the way they do.

Those of you singers new to recording and performing may be wondering how in the world these relationships can be so important. If you fall into that category, picture spending a lifetime working to arrive at the top of your game, only to find yourself at a crucial moment with an audio situation you can't wrap your head around, as well as an inability to communicate what you need to the producers and engineers you're working with.

It happens more often than you think and can cause more problems and career setbacks than you can possibly imagine.

Some Common Problems

Are you ready to lighten up and have some fun? Good. So am I. Here we go.

> "It's like dealing with a child. Only with a child, even *before* they learn to talk you can still actually communicate."
>
> —Steve S., Recording Engineer[1]

> "It's hard enough trying to make it in the music business. But to have all that hard work crumble because some ego-tripping jerk behind a console would rather let you bomb than do his job is unbearable. Even if he's not determined to make you fail, he certainly seems to enjoy watching you fall."
>
> —Michelle P., Recording Artist[2]

Are these extreme examples? Absolutely! Not all singers and engineers are itching to rip one another's heads off. Still, these quotes point to frustrations that even the best performers and technicians have likely witnessed or had to deal with at one point or another in their careers.

Before we dive into the specific issues underlying these frustrations, I'd like to share a few of my own less than ideal experiences, first with technicians, then with other singers. Hopefully these stories will help to illustrate the breadth and scope of the challenges so many of us face.

Producers and Engineers

Producing a Track

A number of years ago, I was doing a good deal of songwriting and had an instrumental piece to submit for a television spot. The song was finished—I simply wanted to have it arranged.[3] Given that it was being pitched as a musical theme for a recurring show, the quality of the finished track was of paramount importance. The deadline was a week away.

An engineer friend, we'll call him Mark, agreed to take on producing the song, but only on the condition that he could be an equal cowriter.[4] While this isn't a standard arrangement with a fully fleshed out song, it is increasingly common that producers will ask for some or even half of the songwriting credit in exchange for the unique sound they will bring to the work. This is particularly true in the pop and urban genres when a producer is well known; partial ownership of a song or its publishing is often traded for the connections a writer hopes the producer's name and reputation will facilitate.[5]

I didn't need Mark's connections for this particular pitch, but agreed to the arrangement anyhow. I was short on time, and while Mark and I had never worked together, I'd known him for years, liked him as a person, and admired his musical abilities and engineering projects (one for which he'd received a Grammy Award).

The afternoon before the deadline to submit the piece, I received the finished track, which consisted of my original piano demo along with the same guitar chord played throughout the entire song. The only other bit Mark had added was a crash symbol at the end of every eight bars.

My first thought was that he'd mistakenly sent over an initial working track. The alternative never occurred to me—that I'd given up a good deal of songwriting credit for two grace notes. And that one day before the deadline, I had nothing appropriate to submit.

Whatever was going on, I figured that we still had an evening to work together to create a product we'd both be proud of.

I was wrong.

When I shared my thoughts with Mark, they were met with shock that quickly turned into anger. I got an earful about how clueless I was about the music business, production, and songwriting. Not to mention how divalike and rude I was to question his choices. He was the producer on this project after all, not me . . . how dare I make suggestions! How dare I insult him this way!

I was baffled, to say the least. And with only an evening to go, I was also uncertain of what to do. In addition to continuing my efforts to communicate with Mark about the track, I made calls to other producers, but no one was able to give me a fast enough turnaround time. I submitted Mark's track halfheartedly and, needless to say, didn't get the project. As for my relationship with Mark, it never recovered.

Mixing a Vocal

Recently, I was hired to sing a demo for a singer/songwriter named Bill with whom I've worked for years. Given that we live in different cities, the music and vocals are recorded in our respective locations and brought together digitally. In this specific case, Bill sent the instrumental tracks to Peter, an engineer I record with often in New York, who loaded them into Pro Tools for me to sing along with.[6] Peter captured my vocals on separate tracks and sent them back to Bill so that the entire song could be mixed by an engineer named Barry whom he had hired.

Below is the e-mail interaction between Bill and myself, unedited, following Peter's sending of the completed vocal files.

---------- Original Message ----------

From: Bill
To: Peter, Jennifer

Hello Peter,

We were not able to finish the mix of Jennifer's new vocal, but we got enough to send to the song plugger.[7] We'll have to revisit this another time and when we do, I'll send you the finished product. Thanks for your efforts, Bill

---------- Original Message ----------

From: Jennifer
To: Bill, Peter

Hi Bill. What does this mean? Is it something on our end that we can fix? Please let us know.

---------- Original Message ----------

From: Bill
To: Jennifer, Peter

Hello Jennifer,

Barry, the engineer, refused to work with me beyond a certain point in the session. He was doing things to your track I objected to and simply threw up his hands and said, "I can't work with you." So, I left. I wrote to him that night and expressed my disappointment and apologized for not making it clear to him at the start that it was my session and I would be telling him what I wanted. He was claiming "artistic and professional right of way." So, I need to either fix that or find another studio. I'm sorry we don't have a finished product but we will. Yours, Bill

---------- Original Message ----------

From: Jennifer
To: Bill, Peter

Bill, I'm so sorry to hear that. If you'd like, please let me know what Barry is upset about. If it's something on our end, of course, we'll try and fix it.

---------- Original Message ----------

From: Bill
To: Jennifer, Peter

Jennifer,

Barry was upset because I think he was over-engineering the track and I asked him to stop. It's nothing you did. Your vocal is great. These engineers always think they can Pro Tools their way to something that has their own signature. Our plugger wanted a more natural, raw sound. In other words, you and the piano. Barry simply forgot who he was working for and behaved unprofessionally. We may talk about you and Peter doing a better mix on your end, but we made it 75% of the way through and as far as I'm concerned, nothing more needed to be done. Chris [the song plugger] thinks it's fine. So, please don't worry. Yours, Bill[8]

Artists and producers often disagree on the "right" way to produce, record, and perform a song. And that's a good thing! Two heads are better than one *because* people see things in unique and different ways.

Too often, however—in the studio and in life—the possibilities of teamwork are trumped by individual agendas, stubbornness, and pride. I can think of countless times when engineers like Barry (as well as singers) have insisted on having their way even when everyone else on a project disagrees. As well as other times when producers have missed, ignored, or overlooked errors rather than put in the proper effort to correct them or admit to their mistakes.

Which reminds me of another story . . .

Working with an Artist

Nancy had spent a couple of years paying her dues in mid-level studios and clubs, and was ready to record an album she could pitch to record labels and promote on tour. It was an exciting step for her, particularly as she was able to hire the award-winning team that produced her favorite singer's records.

Excited as she was, things didn't go well from the beginning. Not only was Nancy unhappy with the vocal takes they were getting, the process of working together was also miserable.

There are of course two sides to this and every story. Three actually, when you consider that no one person or view is entirely objective.

In Nancy's case, however, it turns out that the truth and her version of events were pretty darn close.

The production dream team had earned their reputation working with a very specific type of singer, or rather, a specific kind of female voice—low, rich, and relatively quiet. Nancy had another instrument entirely. And rather than adjust to working with her voice, the producer and engineer expected Nancy and other singers to adapt to the gear, settings, and approach they used with their preferred vocal type. Any vocalist unable to do so was, according to the team, either untalented or too green to know how to work on a major recording project.

Every challenge and issue that came up was therefore immediately blamed on Nancy. This included pronouncements that her voice was "difficult to record, impossible to EQ, and way too dynamic." And not just once; there was an almost hourly reminder that "they had never, ever had this much trouble recording a vocal before." (This turned out not to be true; three other vocalists I later spoke with said they'd had the same troubles and types of interactions with this production team.)

In an effort to deal with her "impossible voice," the duo used a tremendous amount of compression on Nancy's vocal while recording, resulting in constant vocal clipping that made singing and hearing a real challenge. When Nancy brought this to the team's attention, they insisted that the clipping was actually the pedal in the piano track, and that she was imagining things. They then upped the reverb on her vocal in an effort to somehow mask the problem, which only made things worse.

Still unable to get a decent result, they next began to insist that Nancy change her sound. First, to bring down her volume and flatten out her tone and, eventually, to sing every song on her pop/rock record in a breathy head voice. They claimed that this was the only way they'd be able to manage what was "an unrecordable voice."

On the first rough mixes, her voice was unrecognizable in more ways than one. Not only did she not sound like herself, but her vocal was also so far back in the mix that the lyrics were at times indiscernible. This, the producers claimed, was necessary to cover the "ugly, nasal sound they were unable to fix."

How is this a story about *my* less than optimal experience? How do I know for sure what actually happened, and what are all of these direct quotations about?

I was in the studio singing backup on Nancy's project for two days and heard everything firsthand.

Thankfully, Nancy chose my second day to be her last. Good as this move was, she was still unable to leave without getting an earful from the team about how ungrateful, untalented, and impossible she was to work with. One even went so far as to say, "If you leave, you'll never work in this industry again!"

Sadly, Nancy's situation isn't an anomaly; I've witnessed and heard about a number of similar situations. People tend to blame others when they have a problem they don't want to deal with or know how to fix. This production team was no exception.

Unfortunate as the experience was, Nancy's optimism allowed her to view it as a learning experience. Within months, she found another producer and, half a year later, Nancy's first record came out to rave reviews and very much in her own voice.

Singers

If the past three stories shed some light on "technicians behaving badly," these next few should demonstrate that singers can be equally guilty of the same.

Making a Record

A while back, I was coaching a vocalist preparing to record her second album. We'd been working together for a number of months, and both she and her songs were really starting to shine.

While she was vocally ready to go, Mary had previously had less than ideal experiences in the studio and was worried about history repeating itself. She'd long struggled with hearing and singing well with headphones, and therefore asked that I accompany her for a day or two of recording.

In my work as a voice coach, I often go into the studio and on tour with artists. The majority of vocal work is ideally done prior to sessions and performances of course, but occasionally problems arise that are either unanticipated or inadequately prepared for.

At the same time, singers sometimes—generally without knowing it—want a crutch more than they want practical help. I've seen the same type of reliance upon certain friends, specific microphones, alcohol, coffee, and in a session I'll never forget, jelly beans![9]

No matter how prepared you are, or how "reliable" your security blanket of choice may seem, issues come up in the studio. The songs you've practiced so diligently occur differently when technology and anxiety come into play, and it's the work of a professional to anticipate and manage these challenges.

In spite of Mary's prior practice, our work together, and my presence in the studio, she didn't handle the situation as well as we'd hoped. After ten minutes of not finding a comfortable headphone mix or getting a vocal sound she liked, she became frustrated and her mind started working against her.

Rather than stay present in the moment, trust the producer and engineer, and do her best, she deferred to her fears and checked out . . . literally. Twenty minutes into the start of a full-day session, Mary was running down the hall in hysterical tears, leaving three of us on the clock trying to reach her by phone and waiting to see if she would return. She didn't, meaning that she not only lost a day of recording and a good deal of money, but the respect and patience of the audio team as well.

Every session and live experience can be new if we allow them to be. Just like life, each day we are given a blank slate—a fresh page to begin a new chapter. Unfortunately, instead of bravely creating what we want, many of us, like Mary, return again and again to the past, revisiting chapters that we've endlessly tried to turn away from.

Performing and Auditioning

Other times, we find ourselves in entirely new situations and still make poor choices.

Early in my performance career, I did quite a bit of studio work singing demos and background vocals, as well as some shadow tracks.[10] One day, I was recording in a studio where an artist showcase for a major label was to be held. At the last minute, the singer's management decided to shift from an acoustic piano and vocal set to a full band arrangement, and I was asked to step in and sing background vocals for the artist.

As you can imagine, performing for a top industry executive can be nerve-racking, as this one opportunity can lead to the opening of a door you've been hoping to get through for a lifetime. Even singing background vocals, I was nervous being in front of this very important and influential man.

Showcases are interesting. On the one hand, they're intimate, which can make everyone onstage and in the room more relaxed and comfortable. The casual, nonperformance atmosphere often lends itself to conversations and playful banter between and even during songs. I once attended a private showcase where a manager interrupted an artist auditioning for his company to sit in on guitar. Two songs later, other staff members joined in, and the initially acoustic audition turned into an awesome full-band jam session.

At the same time, the intimate setting of a showcase leaves little room for people to hide their feelings. If an artist fails to hook the audience, it's pretty obvious when they start to check out. This can vary from a polite look to a yawn, to glancing at a cell phone and even—and I've seen this happen—people getting up and leaving in the middle of a song . . . even when they, other than the band, are the *only* people in the room!

Unfortunately for this particular showcasing singer, her first impression wasn't a good one, which was a surprise to all of us, including her. Up until that point, she had received nothing but accolades for her vocal talent and performances.

The downside of always being told how great you are is that it's a real shock when you first hear anything to the contrary. "First failures" are always painful, and depending on how you navigate them—in your life and your mind—they can have a lasting impact on the way you experience and express yourself, as well as how you relate to success and failure in the future.

Instead of staying strong and focusing on doing her very best, this singer panicked. Since her performance didn't seem to be working, she tried on sexiness (no dice) and then humor. The latter seemed to strike a chord, and so she grabbed at it like a lifeline.

The problem was that the management company and sound engineer were on the receiving end of that humor.

For the next three songs, this singer not only teased them during the vocal breaks, she invented lyrics about their professional *and* personal failings as well. Gossip and dirty laundry always have their takers, and the executive and his staff were no exception.

Still, as sad as it was that the tactic improved the mood and, it seemed, the label's interest for a while, it was sadder still when the singer failed to realize that her game had run its course. When she did catch on, she made the wrong choice of upping her rude banter, which made the executive's checking out official. The whole thing was painful to witness and uncomfortable to be a part of.

I felt for the singer and still do in writing this today. This was a chance for her to make an important impression, and I understood her panic when things didn't go well. That said, it was a big chance for the manager and sound engineer, too. The willingness to dismiss people so casually in order to achieve your goals—people on your team and on your side who've cared for and made sacrifices for you—is never the right call. This proved to be true in reality as well as in concept; the singer not only didn't get an offer from the record label, she also was dropped from her management contract the next day.

Interestingly, some people get away and even ahead with this type of behavior. I'll never forget the time I went to Memphis to support a friend playing with one of today's top gospel artists. It was destined to be a great night; the singer deserves every ounce of popularity and notoriety she receives for her talent, and her band is one of the tightest and funkiest I've ever heard.

In spite of their incredible performances, I became increasingly uncomfortable during the show. The singer continually interrupted numbers to berate the sound engineer for her inability to hear herself, eventually insulting the man on a personal level as well. Thinking back on it, I'm still not sure what made me cringe the most . . . her slamming the poor guy the entire night, the audience joining in with catcalls, or the look on the engineer's face as he tried desperately to hold the show, and himself, together.

Afterward, I shared with my friend how shocked I was. Was this engineer subbing for the artist's usual guy? Was he having an off night or had they had an argument before the performance?

The answer was no. These two had been working together for about a year. She often treated him this way and he, eager for the paycheck and to be part of such a big star's team, had been enduring her unconscionable behavior the entire time.

Dealing with New Equipment

Not all singers behave so badly, but everyone has their bad days. Goodness knows I've had my share. Here's a particular gem. . . .

About midway through my performance career, I was hired for a rather large and important tour. By that time, I'd had a good deal of experience with most types of onstage monitoring setups and sound systems, and live gigs felt like second nature to me. Even when I couldn't hear myself well, I had learned over the years to compensate by focusing on the sensations of singing, as well as watching and listening for cues from the other vocalists and instrumentalists around me.[11]

When I arrived to rehearsals for the new gig, I was immediately fitted for in-ear monitors, which do a great job of improving hearing onstage by presenting a proper mix directly into the ear and blocking out ambient sound. They are particularly helpful in larger live settings, where distortion, slapback, echo, and the volume of the music and audience can range from distracting to overwhelming.

Great as in-ear monitors are for providing a comfortable and accurate listening experience, singing with them can be tricky. In fact, what makes in-ears helpful also poses their biggest challenge: they don't allow air into and around the ear canal. As a result, they can be particularly problematic for singers who are used to a normal air-to-ear, voice-to-room experience of sound production.

I went into rehearsals with my in-ears excited and with an open mind, yet I found myself increasingly nervous as the performances drew near. Try as I might, I just couldn't wrap my head around how to work with the darn things. Singing with them sounded and felt odd, leaving me without any physical or aural reference whatsoever. As a result, I was not only inconsistent, but there were also moments when I was downright off.

About a week into the gig, my fear really took over, at which point I started blaming the only other person who could possibly have had a hand in my difficult experience: the audio engineer. Rather than take ownership of the situation or, at the very least, manage my reaction to it, I convinced myself and others that he was doing a crappy job . . . an easy persuasion, as most of the other singers were struggling with the in-ears as well.

Locked in the blame game, the energy that could have gone into solving the problem was redirected into frustration, anger, and resentment. I stayed out the contract and was even asked to renew. But I didn't. The experience had been unpleasant, and so had I.

CHAPTER SIX

Communication

Do any of these stories sound familiar? If you're like the majority of people I've worked with, some, if not all, will ring a bell.

Where do these problems come from? And why do they seem so pervasive? What is going on here?!

Common Communication Issues

"How we communicate in the studio can add up to either an amazing soup of creativity, or else massive head-butting where people just don't understand each other and get frustrated. We all hear things differently, and trying to describe those sounds we hear in our heads can sometimes support the maxim that 'talking about music is like dancing about architecture.'"

—Jason Garner, Producer/Engineer, Nashville, Tennessee[1]

While there are a variety of issues that cause problems onstage and in the studio, in my experience communication is the clear winner. To break it down even further, a good number of singers and technicians I've worked with and spoken to about this book insist that certain singers, producers, and engineers:

Don't talk
Don't want to talk
Don't know how to talk
Don't listen
Don't want to listen
Don't know how to listen

Hopeless as this may sound, we're not actually incapable of talking and listening. Ask our friends, families, and colleagues, and I'm sure we'd discover that plenty of both are happening behind the scenes.

Instead, when we work together, there are specific barriers to communication that often arise—to say nothing of the *perception* of barriers—that stem from less than positive past interactions.

Speaking a Different Language

"One singer might respond better to me saying something technical, like 'can you put more of an emphasis on this syllable' or 'pronounce this word this way; it might sing better,' while someone else actually might sing a phrase better if I say 'sing it with more umph.' [Singer/Songwriter] Catt Gravitt was a master at the second kind of more 'ethereal' communication with her vocalists. She would ask a singer to do something using vague emotional language, where I would find myself thinking 'what is she saying?' and then the singer would do exactly what we were looking for! It was a great example of how we all respond differently to different language and communication."

—Jason Garner, Producer/Engineer, Nashville, Tennessee[2]

Have you ever traveled to another country where you were forced to try to communicate with someone you literally couldn't understand? Where, with no other options, you spoke to each other in your respective languages?

I have. Out of sheer desperation in Rome years ago, I was speaking Spanish to a man who was just as insistent on trying to give me directions in Italian as I was determined to understand them. Yet while our hearts were in the right place, neither of us had much to show for our "conversation" at the end of it, save for a great deal of frustration (and in my case a bit of a headache).

The same thing happens to singers and technicians all the time, save for one big exception: they don't know they're speaking different languages!

"It's like, we're both looking at the color blue, but each person sees a different shade. Or an altogether different color."

—Amber Skye, Singer, Songwriter, and Actress[3]

Let's start with engineers. These men and women spend their time in the world of technology, where the intellect plays a leading role. While their work also requires creativity, they deal primarily in numbers, measurements, technical jargon, and the straight talk of "what's so."

Singers, on the other hand, reach for words in an effort to explain physical and sensory experiences that often exist without them. To describe this internal process therefore requires somewhat of a translation, with singers using imagery and metaphors to try to express what they themselves have often never intellectually understood.

When you bring these two "languages" together, you get some interesting cross talk. An engineer wanting to know about the headphone mix might get the response "it sounds too green," while a singer trying to fix what she's hearing might be met with questions about levels of volume, EQ, or compression that make no sense to her.

Understandably, these types of interactions breed confusion, which is only compounded when there is a lack of awareness about how differently they communicate. Both are left feeling that the other person isn't listening properly or explaining things clearly. Or worse, that they're not trying or couldn't be bothered to do so.

Speaking with Different Energy

Another aspect of the language issue deals with *how* singers and engineers communicate. The dispassionate and efficient nature of technology is often reflected in the attitudes of those who use it. No matter how moving a performance might be, engineers and producers learn to remain calm and even-tempered in order to best capture the magical moments.

Meanwhile, singers tend to experience and even require a tremendous amount of passion to create that very magic. It can be a challenge to snap out of the fire and vulnerability of self-expression to talk practically with the production team between takes. Not only because of the consuming nature of performance emotionality, but because these singers are, literally, in another place.

Indeed, just as the languages engineers and singers speak differ, so too do the mindsets from which they are speaking. Technicians work more in what is commonly called the "left brain" or technical mode of thinking, where logic, language, and judgment are paramount. Singers on the other hand move into the "right brain" or creative mode when they're in the zone—a place where time, reason, judgment, and language fade. And as we discovered in *The Art of Singing*, the two modes are experientially about as far from each other as they can be.[4]

This difference is certainly in play when engineers, in their dispassionate effort to tell the truth, call it like it is. After all, "that was flat" is an accurate assessment of what happened when a singer goes off pitch. Why beat around the bush? Time and money are on the line, and professionals who respect one another don't need to use kid gloves.

Yet to singers, this blunt statement is almost always a shock that worsens rather than improves the situation and relationship.

It's not that all singers are sensitive and insecure, or that they can't speak or be spoken to in this candid way; most vocalists can hear and call pitch issues just like a technician.

The problem is that when singers are in the creative space, "flat" doesn't always translate helpfully; they don't necessarily have a reference for how to fix it. What's more, the frank delivery of this technical, value-related judgment can completely pull singers out of the world of vulnerability and creativity in which their best expression and pitch become possible.

That's not to say that an engineer should allow a vocalist to go for hours with a pitch issue unaddressed, or that a singer should use "being in the zone" as an excuse to do whatever she wants. Instead, the solution, as Jason Garner mentioned with respect to his work with Catt Gravitt, is to find a way for the two to communicate technical and creative ideas so that they both get the results they're looking for.

Listening with Different Ears

"A part of me wishes there was such a thing as 'body headphones.' I know it sounds silly, but it's even sillier to think that I can hear all of what I'm singing with only my ears."

—Jennifer E., Singer, Montreal, Canada[5]

Not only do singers, producers, and engineers communicate differently. They hear differently as well—a fascinating distinction I've observed and experienced over the years.

The gist is that while technicians are listening exclusively with their ears, singers "hear" with their entire bodies. Sound, when you're the one producing it, is also *experienced* during the creation process; in addition to hearing the voice, you can feel it as well. And this experience, these feelings, are in many ways as important to singers as the "ear-hearing" that technicians and most people rely upon.

What makes things all the more interesting is that for singers, these equally important notions of hearing, sensing, and feeling often get intertwined and confused. For example, a vocalist might swear that she is hearing something a certain way, when in fact, it is a feeling she's responding to, and vice versa. A note that sounds off to her may actually be an accurate pitch that was generated with a different amount of energy or tension than usual. Similarly, singers will often say that something feels strange when, in fact, it is the pitch that's flat or sharp.

> "The voice is an invisible instrument, it's a mystery. The best science can't explain it completely and still doesn't explain the emotion and personality that move through it. The more I learn about the voice, the more mysterious and extraordinary it becomes."
> —Tyley Ross, Grammy-nominated Vocalist and Broadway Performer[6]

Let's back up a step to understand why this happens. The production of sound occurs thanks to our vocal cords, or vocal folds, which rest in an organ in our throats called the larynx. They're tiny—on average, about fifteen millimeters in length for women and twenty for men. If you're unsure of what your vocal folds look like, imagine your thumbnail divided in two from tip to cuticle and then "unzipped" from the top into the shape of a V.

When breathing, the vocal folds are "open" like this. Connected at the front of the throat (or, in our analogy, at base of the thumbnail), this V shape is their default, resting position, which allows air to flow unobstructed into and out of the lungs. When vocalization occurs, the folds come together and vibrate parallel to each other as air passes through them.[7]

And they do so at very high speeds. For example, to produce the sound of an A above middle C (a note found in the midrange of most women's singing voices as well as in their speech), the vocal folds oscillate at 440 cycles per second.

> "How weird is it to think such a subtle yet complex activity like singing could be controlled by a conscious mind that can only process one or two things at a time?"
> —Bo Seamon, Singer/Songwriter, Austin, Texas[8]

Take a moment to digest that. An "average" spoken and sung note cycles *hundreds of times per second*! The concept is not only virtually impossible to fathom, but one that is also out of our intellectual and to a large extent, direct physical control.

Still, many singers have tried for years to manhandle their voices by tensing their throats and even moving them up and down in an effort to get the notes to do the same . . . in spite of the fact that their efforts are in no way connected to physical or musical reality.[9]

This helps to explain why singers so often confuse feeling with hearing. Many are so used to trying to create and confirm pitches with their throats that when they no longer feel the tension they're used to, they imagine it is the sound that is off . . . even when it's perfectly fine. Just as others may swear that something feels strange, when in fact, it is the pitch that is sharp or flat.

If singers are constantly blurring hearing and feeling in this way, you can imagine how much more complicated things become in the studio. Not often singers themselves, it's understandable why many producers and engineers become confused when vocalists bring up "feeling" in conversations about sound and pitch. Meanwhile, singers are simply trying to communicate about their voices in the only way they know how . . . as they experience them.

To add fuel to the fire, the way technicians talk about sound sometimes makes things worse. By saying that a note needs to be "higher, brighter, or more on pitch," a singer already tensing her throat may do so even more when hearing that a note is "under." Conceptually, these and similar requests are fine, yet the language itself tends to reinforce the unhelpful notions of up and down that generally cause the tensions and pitch problems to begin with!

Listening but Not Hearing

So far, we've talked about problems that, while they occur onstage and in the studio, actually have nothing to do with technology. The same differences would exist in a living room, at a park, or in a car . . . it's just in the nature of how singers and engineers tend to relate to and speak about their respective musical processes.

Now that we have a handle on these differences, we're going to start adding the specifics of technology into the mix. And when we do, whether it's headphones in the studio or stage monitors at a performance, an entirely new dimension comes into play that's often tough for singers to deal with.

While instrumentalists may also struggle with the technological variables of performing and recording, for singers they pose a particular challenge because of a critical distinction between a singer and an instrumentalist: the voice exists *inside of* the singer's body.

Let's understand how this impacts her experience by looking at a typical recording session. When instrumentalists are in the studio, they'll play a piano line or guitar or bass lick and then hear it back in their headphones. Either it's what they wanted to do or it's not. If not, they'll try the pass again, perhaps changing their mental approach to the song, their finger positioning, or the intensity of their playing.

A singer, however, is not only looking for possible adjustments to her mental and musical approach, but for how the instrument itself might need to be adjusted as well.

Often unconsciously, she'll actually try to shift the way she sings—the musculature and process of her sound creation—in order to compensate for what the headphones suggest is missing.

The ability to adjust the vocal instrument isn't in and of itself a problem. As a matter of fact, it is part of what makes the voice so special. As singers, we can bend, stretch, and even go beyond the voice's static physical capabilities in a way other instruments can't.

Still, there is a limit to how far we can bend and stretch our voices. If we stay within those limits, new heights are reached. If we go too far, the instrument itself can break.

Hopefully, this tendency is eliminated early on through instinct or training. To stay vocally healthy, we learn to stay true to the way we produce sound, making minor adjustments to compensate for acoustic differences. An open hall, for example, provides more reverb and a small, carpeted room, a more dull and muted environment.

> "Some people think, 'I should sing louder.' When in reality, we sometimes need more reverb or some other adjustment to hear ourselves more so we don't push over an orchestra in a building with bad acoustics. You need to know to ask for help, and to have the relationship with the sound engineer to be able to do so."
> —Nikki James, Tony Award–winning Singer, from *The Book of Mormon*[10]

When it comes to live performance and recording, however, making these adjustments isn't always as easy as it sounds. For starters, we're not actually listening to our voices or other instruments; through headphones and monitors, we're hearing digital representations of them. And while technology has come a long way, for many singers it can be a challenge to create sound as naturally as they would in an acoustic environment.

The main issue with studio headphones and in-ear monitors is that the partial or total covering of the ear required to deliver an accurate, audible mix, and keep bleed to a minimum in recording, interferes with the normal hearing process so crucial to healthy vocalization.[11] Without the aural perspective of the room, structural voice manipulation becomes much more common.

> "Modern sound design can overwhelm even the unwary vocalist. They can't always hear themselves well, and so there's a tremendous danger of oversinging."
> —Joan Lader, Voice Therapist and Vocal Coach[12]

That's not to say we can't learn to manage these variables. In fact, many singers become so adept at singing with studio and stage gear that they prefer it. This is particularly the case when a recording or live sound engineer is masterful at creating a great mix.

When the mix is off for whatever reason though, even the most experienced stage and studio singers can find themselves struggling. For example, when a singer hears her voice in her headphones or in-ears with too much "high end," her automatic tendency is to darken the tone. Even if she experiences discomfort, even when a producer asks her not to affect the sound, it is often something she can't help. In her ears, she is searching for the sound she is used to—the sound of her own voice—before going after the performance result she and others are looking for.

The same type of unhelpful modification occurs when too much or an incorrect type of compression is used. A singer attempting to increase her volume or energy, but not hearing the results of those increases in her headphones, will push and even strain to the point of pain in a not always conscious effort to create the result she knows she should hear.

For a pianist or guitar player, while poorly set compression levels may result in an unnatural sound in the monitors, they won't so drastically affect the way he plays. Adjustments to EQ will interfere even less so. If the piano sounds too bright or dark, or the guitar too loud, quiet, or lacking in dynamics, it might initially cause a shift in the player's approach, but not at the expense of his technique or the instrument. No one is going to try to bend the piano, stretch the guitar, or cripple fingers in order to get a more authentic sound!

Intellectually, the same is true for singers. They don't deliberately create tension or strain to achieve a great performance. Yet the software and hardware of technology can play with the ears and, as a result, the mind in a way that knocks down the barrier between maximum effort and instrument manipulation, leading to tension, strain, and even damage.[13]

The Communication Choice Point

"The fact is, producers and engineers who aren't singers themselves really have no idea why singing with compression feels different than singing without. Therefore, learning how to identify and effectively communicate the differences between what you're hearing versus what you need to hear is critical."
                                        —Robert Wright, Producer/Engineer, Nashville, Tennessee[14]

A final oddity of headphones and monitors is that they don't always seem to accurately represent what is going on. For a variety of reasons—including congestion, dehydration, the volume being too loud, using only one headphone, or elements in the mix—a singer might be entirely on pitch in her ears, only to head into the control room to hear that she's actually been a quarter tone flat throughout the line.

In moments like these, communication is critical to moving forward productively. Ideally, both the singer and engineer would share what they're experiencing and listen fully and with an open mind to what the other is saying. The engineer might make some changes to the mix, and the singer to her approach. If that doesn't work, maybe they would head out for a break and bit of perspective. Clearly there is a solution . . . they just haven't found it yet.

Without communication, however, the issues we've been discussing escalate into real problems—professionally and personally. To the engineer, the singer was flat. In her ears, she was on pitch. If neither is willing to give up their view, listening stops and stubbornness sets in. Feelings get hurt, stereotypes are reinforced, and the session grinds to a halt.

Self-Revelation Versus Self-Protection

"Intolerance is always a sign of uncertainty and panic."

—Maureen Dowd[15]

When things aren't going the way we want them to, it's easy to take our frustrations out on other people. Particularly when we're unclear what the problem is or how to solve it.

Yet frustration isn't the problem. We all feel frustration from time to time . . . it's par for the course of being human, and certainly part of being in the music business!

Powerful as any of our emotions might be, they aren't the fundamental cause of our problems with other people. It's what we do with our feelings—whether and how we choose to act upon and react to them—that determines the outcomes of our interactions . . . whether we move forward or remain stagnant.

Onstage and in the studio, the real challenge of frustration, fear, and anger is that they tend to lead to withdrawal . . . of our interest, our listening, our kindness, and our participation. Whether for pride or misunderstanding, singers and technicians alike often pull away, determined that they have no choice but to figure things out themselves. This is particularly the case when all "evidence" suggests that the other person has no interest in trying to listen or communicate.

In any relationship, this choice isn't a wise one. Contrary to appearances, there is no power in reactional withdrawal. Even when it's done quietly or gracefully, the sense that one person is right or better than the other lingers, which only harms the situation. This is true even when both people walk away; in reality and spirit, the relationship or incident is left unresolved, only to potentially be re-created in future engagements.

With singers and technicians, withdrawal is particularly problematic, because they can't do their jobs without each other! The relationship is interdependent; no matter how they might feel, they are decidedly in it together for the long haul.

That's not to say it is always easy. As we touched upon in the introduction, singers and technicians generally meet at highly stressful and important moments of their careers, where much is at stake—a meeting that adds additional tension and pressure to any other personal, technical, and communication issues that might already exist.

That's why it is so critical to communicate effectively. When things aren't working, the solution isn't to make the other person wrong and retreat; it is to move closer to each other. Surrender—of wanting to be right, of wanting to be in control—is the key to the spirit of partnership in which the answers can and will be found . . . even in the most frustrating and unfamiliar situations.

For many people, this sounds like a fantasy. Is this type of interaction even possible, much less something we can turn into a regular practice? Absolutely, so long as we're willing to learn the skills of effective communication and commit to using them.

The Art of Speaking, Listening, and Hearing

"The greatest problem with communication is the illusion that it has been achieved."
—William H. Whyte

Effective communication is a threefold process that involves speaking clearly, listening effectively, and hearing accurately. These might sound self-explanatory, but countless communication breakdowns suggest otherwise. Let's take a look at each.

SPEAKING CLEARLY

Speaking clearly, in this case, is not about articulation. It means being certain that what you say is an accurate reflection of what you think and feel. Easy as this might sound, for many people it is a real challenge. Not only are some of us unaware of how we truly think and feel, a host of other factors, including the desire to impress and please other people, influences what we say as well as how we say it.

For example, we may want to say that we're not ready to start working on the next section of a song because we feel we haven't gotten a good take of the current one. Yet in our effort to avoid a disagreement, we might hedge our true intention, saying something that, unbeknownst to us, may suggest a willingness to move on.

The result? Confusion and a breakdown in communication when the person we're speaking to seems to be resisting and even going against what it is we *thought* we said!

The next time you're about to talk, in or out of the studio, take an extra beat or two to make sure that what you're going to say is what you truly want to share. In those moments of reflection, you'll likely find a number of competing personal concerns and professional intentions arise that would usually confuse your message. Deal with each, so that when you do speak, your words are clear as well as accurate.

LISTENING EFFECTIVELY

"Listening we often think of as more passive—important, but somehow lesser or secondary. But listening is the clearing in which speaking can occur—without it, there isn't any speaking."
—Brian Regnier[16]

Our multitasking, rapid-fire culture has left us with very short attention spans, or, at the very least, with less practice paying full attention. Combined with our decreased levels of trust and intimacy, it's no wonder why listening has become a real challenge. We can't or don't maintain eye contact. We hear part of a sentence, think we know where the other person is going, and stop listening (or worse, interrupt and finish the sentence for them). Our minds wander. We lose interest quickly.

Of course, this affects not only the way we listen, but the way the person we're supposedly listening to speaks to us as well. In a cycle, we then go around and around . . . saying something slightly different than what we want to say, not being fully listened to or understood, and then trying to regain the attention we are frustrated to have lost.

HEARING ACCURATELY

Many people think of listening and hearing as the same thing. And while they're certainly related, hearing has to do with far more than whether we pay attention in our conversations and the information we take in.

It has to do with *how* we do both.

> "The time to make up your mind about people . . . is never."
> —Katharine Hepburn in *The Philadelphia Story*[17]

To every interaction, we bring a set of filters. Our thoughts, past experiences, and prejudices . . . our hopes, fears, and impressions of other people and the world around us . . . these filters are with us wherever we go and are always on, including when we're doing our best to listen objectively. Even when we are in total agreement with what someone is saying, even when we like the person immensely, our past experiences and preconceived notions—about them, about the topic, about the environment we're in—are having a say of their own.

It takes awareness and practice to turn down the volume on these filters. When we do, in addition to hearing what someone is actually saying, we have the extraordinary experience of being *truly and objectively aware* of that person. Separate from our past experiences with them, including our certainty that we know their "type" or "who they are," we can receive them and their words without adding meaning of any kind.

≈

Imagine what this threefold approach to communication would bring to our working together onstage and in the studio:

- Using direct, fearless speech; really knowing what we want and how we feel, and having the courage to say what we mean.
- Giving our entire attention to others, and listening until they've fully expressed themselves, and feel heard.
- Having the determination and patience to continue paying attention and listening until we truly understand what other people are saying,

no matter how new, foreign, or even uncomfortable their ideas might be to us.

- Experiencing one another fully and newly; setting aside our impressions and judgments so that new possibilities can be created in our relationships and work together.

What a difference that would make! Frustration and pettiness disappear, along with all of the barriers that once seemed impossible to overcome. We may see—and hear—things differently; we may not communicate the same way. Yet our determination to listen to and understand one another makes it possible to have a successful and positive experience.

CHAPTER SEVEN

Intentions and Expectations

Another big issue onstage and in the studio is that singers and engineers bring with them very different intentions and expectations. Which is intriguing . . after all, don't we want the same thing? A terrific show or recording?

We do. Though we often have differing ideas about the best ways to get there.

A Look at the Differences

Please remember that these aren't hard truths running along a performer–technician divide. They are generalizations I'm sharing to help us unravel unhelpful yet common issues, feelings, and perceptions. Whether you do or don't find yourself in these pages, learning to identify and deal with fixed intentions and expectations is a critical skill in music and beyond. We all have them, and even the subtlest ones can have a powerful impact on our relationships.

Results Versus Experience Focused

> "Another one [producer/engineer] never looked me in the face. He sort of did, but he never talked to me directly. My manager said he was elated, but how the hell would I know that? I thought he wanted me out of there. We couldn't even make a basic connection."
>
> —Amber Skye, Singer, Songwriter, and Actress[1]

The main focus of engineers in recording and performing is getting a great result. It's not only what they're trained and paid to do, but also the nature of their motivation. When all is said and done, the client is expecting a fantastic finished product and it's their job to deliver it.

This focus and results-oriented point of view sometimes leads to soft social skills being overlooked or neglected. The warm and fuzzy, the touchy-feely . . . unless they're serving the session, they aren't a priority for many technicians. And while this may give them the appearance of having thick skin, they're really just focused on being the anchor and driving force of the day's efforts.

Singers, on the other hand, often want and even need a certain intimacy in order to get the results that they and the production team both desire. After all, they're not only dealing with a technical instrument, but also with the mind and mystery that run it . . . a world filled with ritual, emotion, and superstition.

Given the difference in their approaches, it isn't surprising that hackles can get raised. To the singer, this type of engineer comes across as inconsiderate and aloof. How is she supposed to connect and get a great vibe with him that's necessary for her to relax and sing well? Meanwhile, this singer seems to the engineer as if she's more interested in a good time than a good product. She can talk about her feelings and life with her friends later. Now's the time for getting to work and singing.

I've heard both of these sentiments expressed many times. And there is nothing wrong with either their feelings or their approaches; problems only arise when they assume that their way of doing things is right for everyone and take other people's behavior personally. Engineers care about process and personal dynamics, just as singers are interested in the final product and getting it done effectively. They just go about achieving their shared goals in different ways.

Need-To-Know Versus Full Disclosure of Information

"The most important thing you can do as a director is to give a lot of love."
—Josh Charles, Actor/Director[2]

Another common issue involves the type and amount of information that is communicated during the recording process, as well as in soundchecks before live performances. Focused on the result, engineers and producers share thoughts and details they feel will serve to get the job done, sometimes leaving certain things unsaid or glossed over.

Meanwhile, singers generally want the sharing of information to flow freely and fully . . . both ways. To that end, not only will they tend to give more information than the engineer needs or wants to hear about their experience, but may also expect or hope for the same in return.

In addition to wanting his thoughts on each take and step of the process, singers often look for the "why and how" of recording and editing from the engineer. Sometimes they're curious about certain settings or why adjustments are resulting in specific vocal sounds. Other times, their interest is about building trust, closeness, and camaraderie for the sake of the relationship and by extension, in their minds, the result.

Whatever the reason, focused on capturing a great vocal take, an engineer rarely wants to explain the recording process in detail or analyze his feelings about each and every phrase. After all, it's a session, not an audio engineering class. To say nothing of how unhelpful (and uncomfortable) an in-depth chat about the singer's vocal strengths and weaknesses might be . . . in or out of the studio!

Unfortunately, when a producer or engineer avoids certain conversations or deliberately withholds information—even with the best of intentions—the singer is often left feeling like an unequal partner in the process. One who isn't respected or liked enough to be privy to details he appears to feel are above her.

This is particularly true when things aren't going well. While engineers are listening to what is going on moment to moment, they're simultaneously hearing the song or project in their heads as a finished product and may base their communication on what they know it will take to get that result. Sometimes it has to do with the singer's performance and other times with editing and post-production they'll do later on their own. Yet without this reference point, many singers feel lost and frustrated.

Communication and understanding are therefore key. Knowing that a vocalist wants and even needs connection and information, what engineer wouldn't be willing to open up and share a bit more? Knowing that an engineer is as committed to a great result as she is, what singer wouldn't relax a bit and refrain from interrupting his process?

Without communication, however, these situations tend to result in technicians feeling pestered and annoyed, and singers feeling babied and hurt.

Predictable Versus Unpredictable Instruments

Part of why singers want so much interaction and communication with engineers and producers is that they're trying, in a sense, to ground themselves.

What does this mean?

Let's start by looking at things from the technician's perspective. When he walks into the studio, he knows his gear. Using it requires training, experience, and judgment, but there's nothing unpredictable about the equipment itself; he knows how it works and what to expect from it.

The biggest variable producers and engineers have to deal with is the performance of the musicians, and for our purposes, the singer: what she'll bring to the table in terms of her unique instrument, ability, mood, and delivery.

For the singer, the same variable is also true. Yet for her, this variability is the whole picture. While she knows her voice and hopefully a thing or two about recording and live performance, she is working with an instrument that is not entirely consistent from day to day. Certainly she'll do her best, but there is no formula with a guaranteed outcome; her tools don't function exactly the same way, every single time.

The best singers handle this unpredictability with professionalism and maturity. Regardless of how their voices (and the minds that run them) might be behaving on a given day, they make a commitment to give each take and performance their all.

Less experienced or grounded singers, however, often come to the table stressed out and insecure; a state of mind that only gets worse at the first sign of an imperfect note or take.

Many people have a hard time relating to this vocal and personal unpredictability: You chose this career; why does it seem so challenging and uncomfortable for you? Why is there so much drama when you record and perform? If it's so bad, why not just do something else?

Obviously there are many reasons why singers grapple with fear and insecurity in their careers, including those we discussed in the last section. Still, the variability of the human voice can throw even the most confident and grounded of vocalists for a loop. Add to this any relationship, communication, and technology-related issues, and it's no wonder that performing and recording can be so challenging.

A lot of people in and outside of the industry forget this when they're looking at the positives of a performance career. The recognition, the money, the self-expression . . . what is there for singers to complain about?

For better or worse, this is a rose-colored view of an artist's life. Is it exciting? Yes. Is it an honor and a rush to perform in front of people who admire you and your music? Of course. But that doesn't mean it's always a joyride. No matter how professional or prepared you are, it can be nerve-racking to open your mouth and never know for certain what will come out—particularly in high-pressure situations.

Mental Versus Physical Exertion

Another distinction between performers and technicians is the different kinds of energy they use. They may be working side by side in the studio, they may partner to put on a live show, but the two are engaged in very different activities using entirely different sets of tools. And too often, there is neither an understanding of nor an appreciation for all that the other is doing.

These types of energy can be broken down into type, intensity, and duration of effort.

> "One hour onstage is like sixteen hours of manual labor, physically and mentally."
> —Engelbert Humperdinck.[3]

As a nonmusical analogy, I can read a book for up to five hours or so and write for about half that amount of time, but I'm unable to run for more than twenty minutes. Of course, some people can't focus for long periods and others can exercise for much longer. But generally speaking, the human capacity for mental exertion generally outlasts the physical.

Audio technicians tend to fall into the "reading and writing" category. A very specific kind of listening is required, as is the chesslike ability to simultaneously view the project in both a focused and broad context. It's challenging intellectual, technical, and creative work . . . and it occurs primarily in the mind. Which means that in terms of clock hours, technicians can work for longer periods than singers. Fatigue, extra-long sessions, and even a hangover are not ideal for getting any kind of work done, but they won't necessarily hinder their ability to do a great job.

Singers, on the other hand, while dealing with the mind, are also intensely engaged in their bodies. Shorter intervals are ideal and even necessary, as fatigue is evident more quickly with physical effort. And that hangover, as well as any emotional stuff going on, will almost always show up on the recording or live mic, regardless of how professional a singer might be.

Most show lengths and set structures accommodate the endurance capabilities of the singers in live performance, but the same is not always true in recording, where studio sessions are generally booked for a minimum of three hours. Notions of time and performance expectations get collapsed, and both singers and technicians often find themselves frustrated when forty-five minutes will wear a vocalist out.

And the fatigue isn't just physical; having to sing the same line again and again out of context—and being prepared to do so at the drop of a hat after a long wait—is creatively and emotionally demanding as well.

Without understanding the differences in how singers and technicians work, unhelpful expectations can emerge and detract from the quality of sessions, performances, and relationships. Technicians often feel that singers aren't working as hard as they are. They're on-site long before and after singers come and go; all the artists do is show up, sing a little bit (often complaining all the while), and then go home, while they're there all night tearing down the set or rig they spent the whole day putting together, or editing and tweaking endless tracks. From the technician's perspective, singers have it easy!

It's true that singers may not be working as many hours as technicians. But that doesn't mean they're not working as hard! They may not be loading in or testing the gear a half day before the session or show starts, but they're not idle. Singers are spending that time physically and mentally warming up and getting ready to perform. And what's harder, tweaking knobs or carrying the weight of a show or record on your shoulders? Most days, singers would rather hit a few buttons than jump through such shifty vocal hoops and impossibly high performance expectations!

I've heard these and similar comments time and again. Thankfully, like most of the problems and perceptions we've been talking about so far, they have more to do with a lack of awareness and communication than inherent inconsideration or disrespect. The key, as always, is to begin the discussion.

Producing Value Versus Conserving Money

Just as problems with money can lead to the eroding of personal and business relationships, it also causes stress onstage and in the studio . . . a stress that tends to land squarely on the singer's shoulders. Unless an engineer or producer is working on a speculation deal, the singer, her management, or her record label is likely paying for the project or performance, including the technician's time. Which is to say, the money is coming out of her pocket.[4]

We've already discussed the challenges of working in a new environment with new people and technology under the pressure of career-making-or-breaking expectations. Personal and performance fears and insecurities don't help either, adding to a scenario that is already less than ideal for being creative.

Now, imagine how much more stressful things can get when money is on the line . . . minute by minute by minute.

> "Funny how fast that whirlwind of creativity can come to a halt when we're faced with the task of shaping it into something that's ready to be shared."
>
> —Jessica Strawser, Editor, *Writer's Digest*[5]

It's tough to do your best if you're constantly watching the clock to see how long edits, gear transitions, and breaks are taking. A veil of skepticism falls over the scene as many singers, whether they mean to or not, look at everything through the lens of "is this necessary? Is the producer wasting my time, taking advantage of me, or trying to earn a few extra bucks?"

Communication isn't always verbal. We're all aware of the power and impact of critical glances and wary looks, both on the giving and receiving ends. Which is why an up-front conversation about economic and time-management concerns is so important. Without it, it's no surprise that producers can become baffled and frustrated by distracted, irritable singers.

Additional Intention-Related and Expectation-Related Challenges

Preparation

"Being a live theater performer, my first recording studio experience was frustrating. Take after take exposed the pimples and wrinkles that one can get away with during a live performance if they have enough charisma and characterization to take the audience on a journey. I resented the playbacks of what seemed 'close enough for jazz' in my ears, but were flawed in the recording. I couldn't understand why my voice sounded so good live but on tape did not. . . ."

—Vivian W. Kurutz, Singer and Playwright, NYC[6]

On one level, singers are master preparers. A tremendous amount of time is spent training and practicing, and in the case of many recording artists, songwriting as well. In fact, singers prepare physically and mentally for success virtually non-stop, whether or not any performance or recording dates are on the imminent horizon.

Yet as we've discussed, another kind of preparation is all too often neglected, and that is with the technology that makes recording and live shows possible. Indeed, for all of their training and practicing for a performance career, for all of their songwriting and rehearsing prior to recording, singers rarely take the time to proactively work with the technology that facilitates both.

There are a number of reasons for this, including access and money. Not everyone has friends who work in recording studios or have Pro Tools rigs at home. Even fewer people can afford to book studio or stage time to practice, much less to record or perform.

Yet there's more to it than that. There is often an assumption that when the time comes, a singer can show up to the studio or stage and that everything will work out . . . that they just need to sing the way they always have, perform the way they've always practiced, and that the technology and those running it will meet them where they are and ensure that things turn out perfectly.

It doesn't work this way. And with a bit of thought, the reason why is clear: In what other setting, line of work, or discipline can you just show up, with no training or practice, and do a great job? Where else in life can you use an entirely new set of tools competently, much less expertly, without knowledge of how they function or experience with them?

Absolutely nowhere.

It's like expecting to ride or swim perfectly the first time you get on a bike or into a pool. Practice and patience are not only to be expected, they're required to achieve mastery.

Thankfully, access to studios, friends in high places, and deep pockets aren't necessary to gain the skills required for stage and studio singing. With a pair of inexpensive studio headphones, a handheld microphone, an average laptop, and free recording software, we can learn the practical basics of studio hearing and singing. We are able, with the same microphone and a decent amp or pair of speakers, to practice balancing our listening and performing in a live setting (to say nothing of the many free open mic nights available in most cities).

Some singers take these steps but the vast majority do not. This needs to change.

Perspective

When a singer finally does get into the studio to work on a record—hopefully with a bit more technical understanding and experience from here on out!—it's a really big deal. A lifetime has gone into physically preparing for this moment, including years specifically dedicated to the writing, arranging, practicing, and stylizing of these particular songs. Money long saved is now being quickly spent on a product that the singer and her team hope to leverage into opportunities to create or enhance her career.

It is a different situation for the engineer and producer. Yesterday or last week, they finished another artist or client project and soon they'll begin another. Often, they're working on many at the same time.

Certainly they care about the quality of their work and reputations, as well as fulfilling the expectations of their clients. But still, this isn't *their* record. No matter how much they like the artist, how excited they may be about the music, or even how invested they are personally, professionally, and even economically, they just don't have the same amount riding on it.

As a result, some producers and engineers lack the patience and understanding they themselves would be grateful for were it their record, career, and dream on the line. Those who are able to give each project absolutely everything they've got find themselves well rewarded with not only happier artists, but with a far better relationship, experience, and product as well.

Dealing with Intentions and Expectations

To sum up the intentions and expectations we've addressed so far, singers want understanding, partnership, equality, and camaraderie. Their desire for sessions and performances to go smoothly and to end well means that they plan on tracking vocals or soundchecking with the engineer—however long it takes—until things are perfect (in contrast with the great result engineers intend to achieve in a timely manner).

While singers have the intention of doing their best, they aren't always fully prepared to do so vocally, emotionally, or with respect to the technology, or to engage in effective communication if and when things don't go well.

Technicians also have expectations about how they want to be treated and spoken to. They want to be trusted, respected, and allowed to lead the charge of getting the job done, which in their minds requires the singer to show up and sound great (as well as to stay emotionally even).

That said, technicians don't always have the intention of sharing leadership with or responsibility for the singer's performance, both of which require considering what personally or professionally might be missing on their own end in order for the singer to get the results that they're both looking for.

Like all intentions and expectations, there is nothing inherently wrong with any of this. People are who they are and want what they want. Were these dating profiles, each could share their candid desires and then wait eagerly to see if the right fit were to come along.

Unfortunately life, including dating, rarely works this way. We don't live in our own respective vacuums, where our every hope and wish is fulfilled on command by a perfectly matched someone. The stars do align from time to time, but generally, perfect compatibility only happens when one person downplays his or her own desires in submission to someone else.

Think about it . . . should singers be willing to walk into the studio and do whatever an engineer or producer says, even when their instincts say otherwise? How many technicians would do precisely what a vocalist wants when their training and experience suggest it would be the wrong course of action?

Not many, or at least, not for very long. And thank goodness! None of us appreciate having our opinions and desires discounted in the studio, at home, or anywhere else. And as attractive as the idea might be conceptually, the majority of us wouldn't want others to sacrifice themselves and their every hope and dream in order to fulfill our own.

Why then does it seem so hard for people to find a middle ground . . . to come together and bend a bit on what they expect so that everyone gets at least some of what they want?

Because we aren't talking to one another about what we want and expect.

Beginning the Conversation

"One of the most important things that often gets overlooked in the initial meeting is the project's game plan—who's going to do what, who's in charge of what, what duties are included in the price, who's getting writing credit or not for substantial alterations along the way, who's paying whom how much and when it will be paid, etc. It's imperative that everyone knows in no uncertain terms exactly what will be expected of them on a project *before* the project is begun in earnest. That initial discussion establishes the relationship, and the relationship is everything."

—Robert Wright, Producer/Engineer, Nashville, Tennessee[7]

How often do you walk into the studio and share your concerns about money and time management? Do you talk with your audio team about your preferences for how to best communicate with one another before you get started? I imagine that most of you would answer no. And just as in our nonmusical relationships, when we aren't fully up front with one another about what we want, we very often don't get it.

Gaining Awareness

To make things even more confusing, few of us are aware of the many intentions and expectations we carry with us. Think about it: before picking up this book, most of you singers probably thought your only intention in the studio was to sound great and get a fantastic result. Now though, you may see a good number of additional expectations lurking about as well. The same goes for technicians.

Unfortunately, when we are unaware of our intentions and expectations, we're trapped in the bizarre dance of not knowing what we want, but insisting upon it all the same. Which means that our disappointment in not getting our way lands squarely on other people's shoulders, rather than where it belongs: with us—those who created the expectations and intentions in the first place, whether or not we were aware of doing so.

Understanding Attachment

I once heard it said that at their most basic, all upsets are caused by one of three things: not saying something you want to say, not getting something you hoped for, or not achieving something you wished to achieve. I love this idea, because it points to how easily intentions and expectations can lead to disappointment.

That isn't to say that they always result in negative outcomes, or that we shouldn't have them. Intentions are necessary for us to imagine what we want in life, and expectations are how we measure our progress toward what we set out to accomplish. For example, I wanted to write this book and hoped to do so within a certain time frame. And thanks in large part to creating these intentions and expectations, I accomplished my goals.

Yet the creativity and productivity that come from creating intentions and expectations quickly turn into limitations when we are attached rather than committed to achieving them.

What is the difference?

In simple terms, being committed to an intention means creating a plan and being determined to stick with it to the best of your ability. Often the intention is met, sometimes it isn't. When it's not, you would consider what might have been missing, learn from the experience, and, newly empowered, recommit to achieving your goal.

With attachment, on the other hand, while the desire for the intention may be just as strong, the *need* to achieve it often interferes with doing so. Objectivity, flexibility, and creativity find themselves pushed to the wayside as fixation and perfectionism take over.

When writing this book, commitment inspired me to reach my weekly page goals; attachment brought on anxiety when I thought I wouldn't and frustration when I didn't end up doing so. Commitment allowed me to find time for writing when it seemed I didn't have any; attachment led me to either forcing myself to write, which dulled my inspiration, or giving up in resignation for the seeming lack of time.

As you can see, attachment and commitment have certain emotional markers. For me, commitment leads to curiosity, excitement, a sense of play, and determination, while attachment brings about pride, anxiety, fatigue, and competitiveness with myself and others. Some variation on these themes is true for most people, which explains the frustration that so often comes when the expectations and intentions we're attached to aren't met or fulfilled onstage, in the studio, and in life.

And it can be the smallest of things! Expecting someone to hold the door open, intending to go next at the stop sign . . . The sanest of us are often driven mad when we don't get what we want, especially in areas of our lives that are the most important to us: the engineer who not only wants, but *needs* to be in charge of the recording session. The singer who not only hopes, but *has* to sound perfect. Both find themselves disappointed and even devastated when things don't go the way they should.

And therein lies the problem: "should" is subjective. Expectations and intentions, as well as opinions, values, and beliefs, vary wildly from person to person, making it virtually impossible for others to anticipate what it is we expect, much less to fulfill our desires and behave the way we want them to.

Trading Attachment for Commitment

> "Trade your expectation for appreciation and the world changes in an instant."
> —Tony Robbins, Author and Motivational Speaker[8]

Given the anxiety, frustration, and overall ineffectiveness they cause in relationships and beyond, why in the world do so many of us hold on to these types of attachments?

It's not deliberate. As we discussed in *The Art of Singing*, most fears and insecurities, as well as the attachments and fixations they inspire, are remnants of childhood issues that have resulted in a fearful and scarcity-based view of the world. Disempowering though it may be, we're attached to this way of relating to the world and others out of a sense of self-protection. We don't merely want things to be a certain way and to achieve our goals; we need life and people to be just so in order to prove to ourselves and others that we're visible, valid, and worthy.

Of course, our adult minds don't necessarily realize this. While we still feel the anxieties they inspire, the years have helped to translate our fears and insecurities into seemingly logical rationalizations, reasons, and justifications for why we should maintain our scarcity-based beliefs and expectations: people aren't trustworthy, life is hard, work isn't fair. And if we don't keep up our guard, our minds say, we run the risk of being walked all over or taken advantage of by other people.

The Birth of Partnership

In spite of appearances, a look at any great relationship, team, or company proves that this way of thinking is faulty. No one is an island; isolation and ego-driven independence never lead to innovation. Instead, effective leaders seek out participation and even partnership from every member of their teams, knowing that the best ideas are generated when everyone's contribution is welcomed.

> "Leadership is recognizing that we are all one. That every person you lead is as brilliant as you, as talented as you, and has the same capacity for growth and accomplishment. They simply need to be reminded of this fact."
>
> —Vishen Lakhiani, Cofounder of Mindvalley[9]

For those trapped in the scarcity-based attachment model, this sounds like a recipe for disaster. Opening up and being vulnerable leads to backstabbing, infighting, and passive-aggression; the cynic can't fathom any other possible outcome of inviting everyone to share their thoughts and ideas, much less the ownership of an idea or project!

> "Courage is what it takes to stand up and speak; courage is also what it takes to sit down and listen."
>
> —Winston Churchill

Those of you who have spent time in the studio have probably seen this dynamic before . . . partnership being trumped by people holding fast and fearful to their own ideas and pride, determined that their way is the only right way, and scared to be dismissed if others don't agree.

This is more than an unhappy way to work. When our priority is to justify ourselves and remain in control, we spend more time trying to manage and manipulate other people than we do getting things done. The result is that we're stressed out rather than creative, exhausted rather than inspired, and obsessed with perfection rather than productive.

And we're alone, rather than connected.

No matter how brilliant, talented, and wonderful we might be (or think we are), each of us is only one person, who on our best day cannot compete with the combined creativity, knowledge, and experience of a group. If we want to be successful, we have to set aside our egos and insecurities and become willing to partner with others.

Ending the Power Struggles

"The most important single ingredient in the formula of success is knowing how to get along with people."

—Theodore Roosevelt

The question is, how? Openness and trust are not easy pills for many performers and technicians to swallow; so many of us are steeped in self-protection, and constantly on the lookout for the judgment and rejection that are often par for the course in our business.

Under our cautious exteriors, however, there tends to be as much frustration and righteousness as there is wariness and fear. And in spite of how it may seem to us experientially, the former emotions are the true sources of our problems and discontent. They, not the behavior of others, are what lead us into and keep us tethered to power struggles that sap us of our peace and energy.

Let's look at a tennis match as a metaphor. As long as we continue to hit the ball, the game goes on. And in power struggles, we do just that; again and again we return the volleys of other people's desires to be right, to win, and to be in control. Wanting the same, or to prove the error and arrogance of their thinking, we stay with a loathsome situation . . . rather than simply walk away.

Walk away! And let them win? Let them think it is okay to act that way?

Absolutely. If someone is truly a jerk, why would you want to work with that person? If he or she doesn't respect you or value your ideas, why would you want to spend time with him or her?

The answer, of course, is that we're attached to our intentions and expectations, and the people we've met in the course of fulfilling them. As a result, we would rather continue playing what has turned out to be a miserable game than release the racket and find a new one.

"When we are no longer able to change a situation, we are challenged to change ourselves."

—Viktor E. Frankl, Author, *Man's Search for Meaning*[10]

Think back to when a producer last belittled your ideas, dismissed your preferred vocal takes, or didn't hire you. Or technicians, when a singer was rude to you or blew you off. Obviously, it stings when we're treated this way, but the treatment itself doesn't cause us to suffer. That only happens when we allow our expectations of how people and situations *should* be to run the show.

When we stop reacting to and internalizing what other people do, we are left observing . . . just a game. One without any inherent significance or meaning. Whether we hit the ball back or not is then up to us; if we do, the power struggle and suffering continue. If we choose not to, the possibility for a healthy and productive partnership—with whomever we choose—begins to emerge.

Without attachment, we can listen to others objectively, understand their concerns, and communicate maturely about them. Without taking things personally, we can patiently hear through frustration to the core of *their* fears and desires. And then we can decide the best way to move forward, for everyone.

You see, I'm not telling you to surrender your power. I'm telling you that surrendering your struggle for it is the only way to get your power back.

Embracing Co-Creation

Most people are open to a power struggle–free relationship when it is genuinely offered to them. Even those who seem as though they'd rather die than give up scarcity-based, ego-driven ways of interacting will often leap at the chance when presented with a better opportunity.

And who can blame them? Our singer who won't let go of her determination to be perfect and the technician who insists on being in charge aren't happy or fulfilled being that way. They either don't realize that there is another option, or perhaps lack the bravery to take the lead in bringing about that change.

The same is true for all of us. Whatever benefits we think we've gotten from trying to defend and prove ourselves, they are nothing compared to the camaraderie, productivity, and enjoyment that emerge when we become more interested in working as a team toward a goal we envision and create together. When we play this kind of game, our differences fade to the background and our similarities become crystal clear: we all long to be understood and respected. We want to feel fulfilled in our work and to contribute something of value to the world . . . a contribution we can now make together.

CHAPTER EIGHT

Responsibility

The Blame Game

To get rid of our relationship-hindering attachments once and for all, we have to tackle the issue of responsibility. And we'll start by looking what it is not; though to most of us "you are to blame for this mess" and "you are responsible for it" are synonymous, the two are very different when it comes to being empowered onstage, in the studio, and in life.

What do we mean by blame, then? We all know what the word points to: that someone or something is at fault. Whether a breakup, a plunge in the stock market, or a family fight, most people have an opinion about who or what caused the problem.

What's more, blame always has a negative flavor to it. People don't open up their arms and say, "Bring it on!" While many love to give it, we're loath to get it and will do almost anything to keep the hot potato of fault as far away from ourselves as possible.

Interestingly, as much time and energy as we spend aiming and avoiding blame, you'd think we'd be able to recognize it pretty easily. Yet by rationalizing our blaming of others with reasons that they deserve it—as well as making excuses for why we don't—we often miss the forest for the trees.

Another Look at Singers, Producers, and Engineers

To get a sense of how pervasive blame is, let's take another look at the stories from Chapter Six:

1) I certainly blamed Mark for not delivering a track of a quality that I expected; he in turn blamed me for reacting poorly to his efforts.
2) Bill blamed Barry for not listening to his desires for the track, for not doing what he was asked, and for not behaving in a manner he expected; Barry blamed Bill for not appreciating or implementing his own ideas for the song.
3) The production team blamed Nancy for being a bad singer and hard to work with; she blamed them for making it impossible for her to get the results and record she wanted, as well as for insulting her.
4) Mary blamed the sound technicians for the session not progressing in a timely manner; they in turn blamed her for being unprofessional.
5) The showcasing singer blamed a host of variables and people for not securing the interest of the record label (including, possibly, herself); the management and sound team putting on the showcase blamed the artist for her unprofessional behavior.

6) Finally, I blamed the technology and the engineer for my difficulties working with in-ear monitors; he in turn blamed me for being inexperienced with the technology and difficult to work with.

Amazing, isn't it? Even when we think we're recounting facts, our versions of "what happened" are very often laden with faultfinding.

The Fundamental Cause of Blame

"In virtually every human society, 'he hit me first' or 'he started it' provides an acceptable rationale for what comes next. It's thought that a punch thrown second is legally and morally different than a punch thrown first. The problem with this principle is that people count differently. People think of their own actions as the consequences of what came before, they think of other people's actions as the causes of what came later, and that their own reasons and pains are more palpable, more obvious and real, than those of others."

—Daniel Gilbert, Psychology Professor, Harvard[1]

Blame is everywhere in life. It's not just the singer without a record deal because her producer did a bad job or the engineer who was fired from the touring gig because the artist doesn't know anything about sound. It is also the woman who swears her life is the way it is because of her mother and the man who insists that his family is the reason he doesn't have the money or the drive to go to college. It is the employees blaming their boss for not getting the promotions or pay they deserve and the employers who say that their staff is at fault for diminished profit margins and productivity.

Like winning and being right, as we saw in the last chapter, blame is always about some measure of good and bad. It is based on our personal and cultural sense of how things, other people, and the world *should* be. And when they don't measure up according to our standards, blame arises and persists.

Fair or Unfair?

But what about when it is the boss's fault that I didn't get the promotion? What about when parents and schools actually do a terrible job? And how about the silly and unprofessional behavior of all those people in Chapter Six, as well as the rest of the music business? In these and similar situations, isn't blame not only fair, but justified?

For many, the answer is yes. It seems more than reasonable to assign blame when people don't behave the way we think they're supposed to or when life isn't fair. How else do we know whom to trust or what our next steps should be?

The problem with this way of thinking is that "fair" and "right" are rather fluid concepts, depending on the person experiencing the situation and the environment and culture in which we find ourselves.

"There are many kinds of truth. Of course, there are factual truths; we all know a lie when we see one . . . but much of life is an interpretation. There's a subjectivity to life. Life is not just an accounting of facts, it's how you explain those facts, how you interpret them."

—Yann Martel, author, *Life of Pi*[2]

For example, according to two of Asia's more prominent forms of psychotherapy, Morita and Naikan, the idea of blaming your parents for anything is illogical. In fact, both insist that complete psychological cure from fear, pain, and anxiety comes from dwelling on the following questions about anyone you feel has wronged you:

What did that person do for me?
What did I do for that person in return?
What trouble and inconvenience did I cause that person?

It's quite a different paradigm than the one we have here in the West!

Because ideas about right, good, and fair are largely subjective, it is not a question of whether we *should* blame others, even when most people would say it's clear that we are entitled to.

The *better* question is what it costs us to do so.

For starters, blame leaves us defensive and reacting to the world around us. With our thoughts, feelings, and behavior dependent upon what other people do and say, we're not free to live our lives fully.

What's more, illogical as it may seem, blame keeps us rooted in the very situations and relationships we're so unhappy with and want to get away from.

Resistance and Persistence

Carl Jung's expression "what we resist persists" is famous for good reason: we can only create what we want in life if whatever came before is truly out of the way. Otherwise, we'll meet our past in our present again and again. It's like trying to get away from a bad situation you're tethered to with a rubber band; the harder and faster you run, the more certainly you'll end up right back where you started.

You've practiced endlessly for your studio session, yet you know something is going to go wrong with the production. . . . You're determined to meet the new artist with an open mind, but you're certain of how she's going to behave, eventually. . . .

"People generally see what they look for, and hear what they listen for."

—Harper Lee, from *To Kill a Mockingbird*[3]

The worry and wariness that stem from past experiences not only have an impact on our expectations, but on our present-day energy and behavior as well. Regardless of how hopeful and optimistic we may try to be, our lingering concerns are not only apparent, but actually help to re-create the very realities we're trying to avoid.

So what is the alternative? To let people off the hook who don't deserve to be forgiven? To pretend people are going to be great when they never are? This doesn't sound empowering, it sounds stupid!

Like power struggles, the alternative to blame is not living in denial. It's not about rolling over and playing dead, letting people get away with murder, or inviting them to walk all over us. It's about deciding which you would prefer: to blame or to be empowered in life . . . to react to or to create it. To find fault with people and the world, or to get what you want with both.

> "Between stimulus and response there is a space. In that space is our power to choose our response. In our response lies our growth and freedom."
> — Viktor E. Frankl, Author, *Man's Search for Meaning*[4]

If you're interested in power, creativity, and results—and having relationships that work—you must let go of blame, including all of the wrong-making and resentment that come with it.

That's not to say that it's easy. Here in the US, we are experts at blame, so much so that we often confuse it with insight and wisdom. Indeed, unlike Morita and Naikan, a great deal of our Western therapies focus on how our pasts and the actions of other people have influenced who we are.

Certainly these types of insights can be useful, as they help us to understand the roots of our current beliefs and behaviors. Yet all too often we don't go the distance, from awareness, to understanding, *to freedom*—a full evolution that only happens when we let go of blame and choose instead to be responsible for ourselves and our lives.

The True Nature of Responsibility

> "Who stops us from being free? We blame the government, we blame the weather, we blame our parents, we blame religion, we blame God. Yet who really stops us from being free? We stop ourselves."
> —Don Miguel Ruiz, Author, *The Four Agreements*[5]

Unlike blame, which focuses our attention and energy externally onto others and life, responsibility means having the willingness to own whatever happens to us. To claim it, so that we can gain power in the situations we are dealing with.

To be clear, responsibility doesn't mean that we can control everything that happens to us, that everything that happens is our fault, or even that we condone all that other people do or say. If you'll notice, these statements stem from notions of should, good, fair, and bad . . . a world we leave when we explore the true nature of responsibility.

The kind of responsibility I'm talking about is not about should, good, or bad. It is not about fair or unfair. It is not about right and wrong.

It is about accepting things the way they are, and the way they are not. Nothing more.

Acceptance

If you look at what most of us do, however, we not only do not accept . . . we come up with a whole drama around what it means that things happened a certain way: we are who we are because our mother did this bad thing . . . we don't have what we want in life or love because of that wrong and unfair situation.

I don't have my record deal because I don't have a lot of money or know anyone. I don't get to go to the best auditions because my agent isn't making me a priority.

What happens to us in life has an impact, of course. But to blame other people and life for why things aren't working after—and often, *long* after—the fact is not about dealing with the impact. In these situations, we are allowing blame to disempower us by using it as an excuse to not fight for what it is we say that we want, *regardless* of the circumstances, *regardless* of what people do, *regardless* of what happened and happens to us.

When we accept all that has come before—that it simply is—we cut the cord of "because." Instead of not having a record deal because of someone or something, we simply don't have a record deal . . . period. Or a job. Or a relationship.

By clearing the past through acceptance, we also clear the reasons and the excuses that have prevented us from moving forward and getting what we want. We're then in a position of tremendous power, free to take inspired and relentless action in our careers, relationships, and lives until we either get what we want or feel at peace that we have given it our absolute best shot.

The question, then, is how do we get to this place of acceptance, beyond words or ideas?

Forgiveness

> "Forgiveness has nothing to do with absolving a criminal of his crime. It has everything to do with relieving oneself of the burden of being a victim."
>
> —C R Strahan, Artist and Author[6]

I once heard that refusing to forgive someone is like drinking poison and expecting the other person to get sick. Take a look at your own life and see if this isn't the case in some of your relationships.

When we're in the world of blame and judgment, forgiveness can seem like an awful and even dangerous idea, particularly for those who've endured abuse, pain, and loss. How can we forgive people who have done terrible things to us? Isn't that essentially like opening the door to allow them to hurt us again?

> "The weak can never forgive. Forgiveness is the attribute of the strong."
>
> —Mahatma Gandhi[7]

Forgiveness doesn't mean that we condone what has happened. As Gandhi said, the ability to forgive is not a sign of weakness; it means that you are strong enough to release the grip you've allowed people and situations from your past to have on you in the present. It is a gift of freedom you give to *yourself* . . . the very gift that allows for an acceptance of all that has come before.

So that agent stopped working on your project because you wouldn't sleep with him . . . So a producer signed you to an exclusive deal and then didn't deliver on his promises.

So . . . so what?!

> "You can have results or excuses . . . not both."
>
> —Unknown

When you forgive people for what has happened, you're not saying that they were right. You're freeing yourself from the drama of the situation so that *you can get on with your life*. Without the distraction of blame, you are now able to see clearly, allowing you to be more objective and wise in your decision-making going forward. The sky again becomes the limit on what is possible because the blame-filled past, along with all of the anger and resentment that come with it, are no longer holding you back and dragging you down.

Radical Responsibility

Regardless of how liberating and empowering it might be, choosing this kind of responsibility for ourselves and our lives is nothing short of radical. It means—gulp!—that we are forever giving up our right to being a victim. Instead of blaming others for our problems, it means that from now on we take ownership of them, accepting and forgiving whatever comes.

What's more, with our focus no longer turned outward, we are able to recognize that our own words, deeds, and actions have also had an impact. And to see, with sometimes painful clarity, our own hand in creating and perpetuating the life that we live.

Uncomfortable as it may seem, this kind of responsibility is not "a burden, a liability, or an obligation," contrary to many a dictionary definition.[8] It is an opportunity—the only real opportunity to gain freedom and power in our lives. Not to control all that happens to us, but to have response-ability: the ability to choose our responses and reactions in the face of whatever comes.

> "We must all suffer one of two things: the pain of discipline or the pain of regret or disappointment."
>
> —Jim Rohn, Entrepreneur, Author, and Motivational Speaker

If you're wondering how taking responsibility for everything that happens to you can possibly lead to freedom and power—and what any of this has to do with recording and performing!—here's the answer: without taking responsibility, we always have an "out." When things get rough, when we get tired, when other people piss us off or make mistakes, or when things seem to take too long, we give ourselves permission to quit. We allow time, circumstances, challenges, and our feelings to become the excuses that thwart our intentions, to go back on our commitments, and to stop the forward action in our lives.

When the going gets tough, the ability to walk away might seem like freedom. But ask anyone who has ever quit or given up, and they'll tell you this isn't the case. Regret is the bitterest of pills; the frustration and ache of dreams unfulfilled and chances not taken are always far greater than any amount of energy you could have spent in the first place.

And make no mistake. Without radical responsibility, anything and anyone can step in and steer us off course from what it is that we want . . . even from our most sincere passions, hopes, and dreams.

You say you want to be a successful singer and will do anything to achieve that goal . . . Well, what does anything mean? Up until what point? How able are you to let go of the ideas, beliefs, and pride that keep getting in your way? How long and how hard are you willing to fight for what you want? In the face of how many rejections and criticisms? In the face of what circumstances, challenges, types of people, and obstacles?

A fantastic career, a great relationship, personal fulfillment . . . these things are available to each of us . . . and they often take more effort, time, energy, patience, and resources than we bargained for. Which is why radical responsibility is so important. Without it, blame, excuses, and reasons wait right at our door, giving us the ultimate trump card when things start to seem impossible.

With radical responsibility, however, we are not only able to handle frustrations and disappointments, but also to embrace them—to know and expect that they'll come, and to remain laser focused on what we're committed to all the same. From this vantage point, we acknowledge that we're willing to do whatever it takes and follow through regardless of what life, other people, and even we in an overwhelmed moment might have to say about it.

The Fulfillment of Partnership

The benefits of taking responsibility are just as powerful in groups as they are in our individual lives. In fact, radical responsibility is the ultimate key to ensuring the success of our relationships and the results they generate. Beyond communication and co-creation, it is what fully enables the success of our working together onstage, in the studio, and beyond.

No matter how determined we are to have great communication, we can get by without a true commitment to it—we can stop listening when we don't like what we hear; we can defer to arrogance, judgment, and pride when things aren't going well. The same is true for cocreating intentions; we can share great ideas even if we're not 100 percent dedicated to following through on them; we can quit and walk away when situations don't measure up to our expectations.

True responsibility, however, is an entirely different matter. Regardless of our thoughts and feelings, regardless of whatever unexpected obstacles might arise, our full participation is nonnegotiable. We are either in it for the long haul or we're not.

When everyone involved—whether in a family, community, or in a work dynamic—chooses to be 100 percent responsible for whether things get accomplished as a matter of their own integrity and self-expression, some rather magical things begin to happen:

- **Accountability**: Instead of being on the passive and receiving end of how things normally go in life, whether by default or in an effort to avoid the "burden" or "weight" of responsibility, we now get to claim ownership of their creation. What's more, we get to have a say together in what we can count on and be counted on for. And to experience the joy, empowerment, and freedom that come from fully participating.
- **Resourcefulness**: The fears, frustrations, and doubts that plague the nonresponsible experience dissipate. In their place arises resourcefulness, one of the most underestimated and important creative entities in music and beyond. It causes the energy in the room to shift and ideas and ingenuity to flood in, bringing resolution to the many seemingly "impossible" problems and dynamics with which we've been struggling.
- **Leadership**: Responsibility also allows our notions of leadership to shift from something a single person possesses to a shared phenomenon. Rather than trying and even fighting to determine who is in charge, we can now discover how to best work together, utilizing everyone's strengths and expertise so that as a team we can create and express ourselves in a way that exceeds what could ever have been possible as individuals.
- **Relatedness**: We learn to not only embrace and share real power, but also the meaning of "no one wins until we all do." As a result, we learn to contribute to other people, and to be contributed to—a tremendous experience in relationships of any kind. Confidence, comfort, and creativity emerge when this kind of safety is present, as do trust, respect, and understanding.
- **Generosity and Graciousness**: Finally, with nothing to defend any longer, no need to be right or in charge, we become gracious and generous. We have the privilege of knowing how wonderful and empowering it is to put others before ourselves, and to experience the world as a truly abundant place.

Partnership Onstage and in the Studio

"While an engineer may EQ a voice to get a specific result, I encourage singers to learn how to adjust their vocal sound before it hits the microphone. When you learn which vocal exercises give you your best sound, you are no longer dependent on the potential shortcomings of the recording process. I recall one instance where an accomplished singer who knew my client's voice exclaimed, 'That is the best I have ever heard him! What effects did you use?' And my answer was: 'I didn't use any effects, I just taught him some vocal exercises!'"

—D. Bruce Moore, Singer, Voice Teacher, and
Recording Engineer, Winnipeg, Canada[9]

As a singer, my friend Bruce wrestled for a long time with how to best prepare for recording sessions. Yet no matter what he tried, issues with the EQ in his headphone mix caused him to manipulate his voice and sound production.[10]

Rather than get frustrated and blame technicians or technology, Bruce decided to take ownership of the problem. Focusing on what he could be responsible for, he realized that with practice, he could EQ his own voice (manipulate the highs and lows) without interfering with his technique and performance, thus sidestepping the need for a great deal of digital manipulation on the part of the engineer.

But he didn't stop there. After mastering this skill, Bruce taught other singers how to EQ their own voices, and even became a recording engineer in order to more fully understand how the system as a whole operates. This eventually led him to create a series of tools that make working (together) in the studio easier and more effective for singers and technicians alike.

Take his muffle box for example, which beautifully combats the "mastering the space" issue we discussed in *The Art of Singing*, which we'll touch upon again in Chapter Twelve: singers tend to prefer performing in large, live spaces, where their voices sound most vibrant and natural, yet the ambient noise and echo interfere with an engineer's ability to make a great record. The standard solution is for singers to perform in a sound booth wearing headphones, in which they can hear as much volume and reverb as they desire.

Unfortunately, even with a great live-sounding mix, many singers struggle with the disparity between what their ears and their eyes are telling them. Standing in a small, padded space, many can't help but to pull back and alter their vocal performance in an effort to accommodate the room and the close proximity of the microphone.

Enter Bruce's muffle box. This two-by-two-foot lightweight square of sound-proofing material holds the microphone in its foot-deep, hollowed-out center. The dense padding on every side deadens any ambient noise the microphone might pick up, allowing the singer to be in as large of a space as she wishes. What's more, the visual break of the top of the box means that the microphone isn't directly in her line of sight, relieving the common tendency to focus on and physically compensate for its proximity.

Another incredible benefit of the muffle box is that it renders headphones unnecessary for singers who struggle with them. Instead, small speakers placed at strategic angles behind the muffle box allow them to sing along with a track while preventing any of its sound from being picked up by the microphone.[11]

The ingenuity of both vocal EQ-ing and the muffle box came out of a desire for partnership. Beyond his wanting to fix a problem, resourcefulness allowed Bruce to come up with a Third Best Option in each case; a win-win scenario that other singers and engineers might not have even looked for, much less have believed possible.

Equality and Leadership

Thanks to radical responsibility, like Bruce, we too can go beyond the normal and accepted ways of doing things—the "it's fine the way it is" attitude—and make a real difference for other people, and as a by-product, for ourselves as well.

Still, some habits can be hard to break, especially when deadlines approach and tensions mount. Who is ultimately responsible for the session or gig? Who is to blame for things not going well? And on the flip side, who gets the credit when they do? We're so used to having one person at the top of the "in charge" pyramid that the idea that we can all be responsible *and* successful can take some getting used to.

There are also some rather subtle issues involving leadership and equality that can prove equally challenging. And sometimes even more so, as they're often hard to detect.

Defusing the "Home Turf" Advantage

"When I walked in, the engineer immediately reached for the stereo piano tracks and started preparing the session while I was talking to him. Instantly, there was an urgency about what I was saying because I could see he was already on autopilot even though he didn't yet know what I wanted. He was already in another world. His world."

—Will Safron, Singer/Songwriter, Virginia[12]

I have always marveled at how positive of an effect the home court or home field advantage can have on a sports team, both physically and psychologically. On the verge of a loss, fan support can rally the spirit of a team that's fallen behind and help them to make a comeback. The mere knowledge that they are home has been shown to measurably increase a team's energy levels when most needed, just as heckling can thwart the playing of a vastly superior visitor.

While not often considered, a similar psychology often applies in recording. Unless a singer has her own studio, the majority of sessions occur in spaces owned or rented by the production team, giving them a greater sense of comfort and confidence than the "visiting" singer.

It's important for technicians to become aware of this discrepancy and for vocalists to realize the impact that it can have on their performances, so that the playing field can be leveled.

Learning to Call the Shots

When we're sharing leadership, it's still often helpful for one person to take the lead in determining the logistics and flow of a session or performance: In what order and how long will we work on recording sections of a song before we move on? How much leeway will the sound engineer have to make level changes once the show has started?

Even when the team is in agreement on who's in charge, tension can still creep in during high-pressure situations. "We've already got that take, let's move on" by an engineer, and a singer's "I can't get into the chorus right now, let's get the verses first" are perfectly fine statements. Though in the heat of the moment, the tendency to misspeak and misinterpret is more common, and direct communication can come across as belittling or disrespectful.

We all know that it's not only what we say, but also how we say it that matters, so make sure to take extra care with your communication in these kinds of situations. Even simple and well-intentioned statements can inadvertently have, or be interpreted as having, edges that cut.

Understanding Ownership

While details of rights and usage ought to be discussed before sessions and shows begin, they often remain unclear, particularly with singers new to recording and the business-related aspects of the industry.

Having paid a fee, many singers assume that any recordings of their sessions or live performances are theirs to keep. This isn't always the case, however, as what is often being paid for is the venue and personnel's time. The recordings and masters may be another matter, owned by the engineer or producer and not released without additional payment or conditions. These include consent for usage rights and fees, which help to ensure that a singer will be compensated if and when her vocal (for example, on a demo) is used commercially, and that engineers and producers receive remuneration for the later sale or promotion of demos or remixes.[13]

Even when details about ownership and rights are established up front, a lingering sense of inequality and discomfort can remain depending on who owns, or wishes they owned, the recordings. Regardless of who ultimately walks away with them, it's important to make sure that the working experience is unaffected by these details, which means continuing to communicate and possibly even negotiate until all parties are able to move forward as a team.

Eliminating Passive-Aggression

"It's amazing what gets accomplished when people actually sit down and say the hard stuff."

—Georgia Middleman, Singer/Songwriter, Nashville, Tennessee[14]

In leadership and beyond, being willing and able to speak the truth, as well as hear it, is a critical key to healthy communication. Being responsible doesn't mean holding back what we think in an effort to help things move along smoothly; being a team player doesn't mean hiding what we want in order to avoid rocking the boat. Unspoken communications tend to fester and find their way into the space one way or another, so it's always in service of yourself and your relationships to speak openly and honestly.

> *"Why don't you tell them the truth? Say what you want to say and let the words fall out. Honestly, I want to see you be brave."*
>
> —Sara Bareilles, from *Brave*[15]

For some of us, it takes a lot of bravery to share our thoughts, feelings, and ideas, especially when they may not be met with the reaction we are hoping for. Wanting to please and keep things positive lead many of us to develop the habit of shutting down when presented with the opportunity to speak the truth.

As uncomfortable as it may be, the practice of expressing ourselves powerfully—and training others to hear our voices in this way—is well worth the effort if we want to have equal and productive relationships. This includes being respectful of the fact that people might not agree with what we have to say. Disagreement in and of itself isn't painful; in fact, it is the gateway to learning and growing, whether or not we end up seeing things eye to eye.

CHAPTER NINE

Personality

Habits, Patterns, and Moods

"The only thing you have to offer another human being, ever, is your own state of being."

—Ram Dass, Author, *Be Here Now*[1]

It is so easy to buy into the illusion that external events and issues bring out our worst—that our internal states are merely reflections of what's happening "out there." That we're empowered until we walk into *those* types of situations . . . we're happy until we have to deal with *that* kind of person.

If you've read this far, you now realize that I don't believe this to be the case. After living in the world of responsibility for a while and owning your reactions to everything and everyone around you, it becomes clear that random people and incidents aren't the source of our problems. That in fact, it is the unhelpful patterns in our *own* behavior that cause the majority of poor dynamics we have with other people, as well as many of the frustrating circumstances in our lives.

Again, I'm not saying that abuse, neglect, and trauma do not have an impact. Of course they do. The point, rather, is that by taking radical responsibility for our lives, we get to reclaim our power by determining how we will react to what has happened in the past, as well as in our present day relationships and circumstances.

As I mentioned in the introduction, healthy skin isn't sensitive. It's only when we've been injured that we resist or react to someone's touch. Our wounds cause us to exist in a state of heightened awareness, looking out for danger at every turn, even in places it doesn't exist.

The same is true in our relationships. Other people don't *do* things to us in our conversations. Instead, we are triggered by those who touch our "sensitive spots" simply by being who they are. And when they do, we react in preprogramed ways based on our past experiences and relationships.

What do these preprogrammed reactions look like? Take a look at the list below and see if you can't identify some of your own familiar go-to mechanisms:

Resentment	Insecurity/Self-Deprecation
Making Assumptions	Fear
Haughtiness/Condescension	Skepticism/Cynicism
Being Overly Positive	Humor
Defensiveness	Anger
Arrogance	Pridefulness

Indifference	Aggression
Confusion	Brownnosing
Passive-Aggression	Rigidity/Inflexibility
Pleasing	Being Overly Sweet
Withdrawal	Sarcasm

If you still believe that other people's behavior causes us to react in these ways, consider that two people can have very different perceptions of and responses to the same experience. Just as plenty of singers and technicians can work together in less than ideal situations and come away feeling unaffected and at peace.

The reason for this is that our habits, patterns, and moods are less inherent aspects of ourselves, and more traits that we've picked up as a way of coping with life and other people. Some work for us, others don't. The trick is to figure out which is which, and to start untethering yourself from the latter.

The Personality Principle

Background and Development

"It is our choices that show what we truly are, far more than our abilities."
—Albus Dumbledore in *Harry Potter and the Chamber of Secrets*[2]

There has been an ongoing debate about the development of personality for decades, and whenever you're picking up this book, it is likely still going on. Is personality a function of our biology or of our upbringing? Perhaps a bit of both?

In the nature versus nurture debate, both sides have their merits. Yet in my experience, first as a performer, then as a coach and counselor, I've come to believe that while genetics certainly have a hand in the construction of our personalities, our experiences in and of the world are as powerful, if not more so, when it comes to their development.

If this is true, it's great news! It suggests that there is flexibility in who we become; that not only what happens to us, but our reactions to our circumstances play a role in which of a variety of ways we might turn out and interact with the world.

While it is awesome to think that we may have such a powerful say in who we are, it appears that these personality-defining moments often happen when we are very young and unaware that they are occurring. The young child of divorcing parents who becomes a "good boy" in order to try to keep his parents together might years later take for granted his pleasing and organizational tendencies as "who he is." The girl who felt excluded in elementary school and gained approval when she made jokes, as an adult believes herself to be innately funny.[3]

"The greatest discovery of any generation is that a human can alter his life by altering his attitude."

—William James

Interestingly, when we come of age and can gain an awareness of these decisions and their results, we rarely recognize them for the person-shaping events they were. We *know* ourselves to be a certain way and can't imagine a time when we weren't funny, organized, or people-pleasing. And we go through the rest of our lives gathering evidence that confirms the constructed truth of who we believe ourselves to be.

In my practice over the years, I have seen many of these decision-based personality manifestations. And in my work with young performers, this includes while the process is happening in real time. Often, I've had the great fortune of being able to intervene so that reactions to home, school, and professional circumstances remain just that. Other times, I have been left to observe as events led young singers to take on personas that from then on they believed to be inherent parts of themselves.

Singers and Engineers

"We are what we repeatedly do. Excellence, then, is not an act, but a habit."
—Will Durant

Just as I don't think that people are genetically predestined to be funny or people-pleasing, I don't believe that there is an inherent performer or technician type. Rather, I believe that the experiences we have and feedback we receive shape who we are, including our career choices and professional interactions.

For example, the child who gets constant validation from family, friends, and community for her voice learns to extend outward for approval and accolades, while another who receives positive feedback for being thoughtful and independent starts to nurture introspection. Somewhat practiced in extroversion, the young singer makes friends easily and engages in activities that keep her in the spotlight, while our budding technician excels by quietly reasoning and creating music.

Following these two through school, we can see how the singer, bolstered by what others think of her and her voice, might start needing the attention and approval she used to merely desire. And how the technician, having cultivated a rich inner life, could find himself on the social outskirts and choose to remain there so as not to chance rejection.

It's not a surprise that she would become outgoing, emotional, and expressive, and he more practical and reserved. Their challenges are somewhat predictable as well: our singer's fear of inadequacy might express itself in neediness and sensitivity, while for our self-developed technician, arrogance and defensiveness would perhaps be more common.

"When I let go of what I am, I become what I might be."
—Lao Tzu

Obviously, these are two of countless different paths singers and engineers can take. I've known vocalists and instrumentalists who are introverted, intellectual, and technically minded, as well as producers and engineers who are emotional, extroverted, and intuitive. Many more are a blend of the two.

That said, for whatever reason, close variations on these themes do show up regularly in the lives of performers and technicians I know and have worked with:

	The Singer:	The Engineer:
Childhood	Extroverted	Introverted
Teens	Popular but Insecure	Unpopular but Superiority Complex
Personal Victories	Attention	Intelligence
Biggest Fear	Failure	Rejection
Sense of Meaning	Approval	Respect
Language and Learning[4]	Right Brain (Artistic)	Left Brain (Logical)
Affect	Expressive	Reserved
Mentality	Intuitive	Intellectual
Intelligence	Emotional	Practical
Relatedness	Inclusionary	Exclusionary
Success Conditioning	Being "Perfect" (Idealistic)	Being "Right" (Realistic)
Communication Desires	To be flattered, heard, and acknowledged	To be admired, trusted, and respected
Adverse Coping Mechanisms	Feelings of Inadequacy	Feelings of Insecurity
	Highly Sensitive	Highly Defensive
	Elitist, Patronizing	Condescending, Dismissive
	Overly Emotional	Easily Angered

Responsibility and Flexibility in Personality

"If from now on you will treat everyone you meet like a holy person, you will be happy."

—Susan Trott, Author[5]

If there are no fixed performer and technician "types," why bother sharing this list? Because awareness is power. Whatever our and others' personalities may be, whether we *are* or have *become* that way, having a sense of what we may encounter in the people we work with prepares us to more effectively partner with them, as does choosing to be responsible for the impact of our own ways of being on others. What's more, understanding that there are reasons for who each of us has become allows us to bring compassion and flexibility to our interactions, further helping us to shape their outcomes for the better.

Producers tend to be great role models in this area. Are they naturally a blend of these performer and technician personality types? Or do they learn out of professional necessity to get along with both? Who knows . . . it varies from person to person.

That said, we all rise to the challenges we either want or have to face. Producers wouldn't get very far in their careers if they were constantly rude to the singers they worked with, or obnoxious when engineers didn't work fast enough. We're social creatures; we learn to behave the way we must in order to get what we want. For producers, being a team player is a requirement.

Singers and engineers aren't quite there yet, as a host of "bad behaviors" are not only tolerated but also often expected. Still, we can continue turning the tide on the status quo by being responsible for and making changes to our own behavior, as well as expecting the best from and nurturing the best in others.

PART THREE

Mastering the Tools

CHAPTER TEN

An Overview of The Recording Process and Pre-Production

"If you can't explain it simply, you don't understand it well enough."

—Albert Einstein

Many of us remember high school science and math as anything but simple. For me, classes in both brought about a sense of dread and long hours into the night trying to wrap my head around seemingly mind-bending concepts.

Music theory is similarly challenging for musicians at every age and stage. Even those with a great relationship with their instruments often find themselves at a total loss. Countless others feel that by attempting to learn the theory, they will somehow detract from their creativity and performing.[1]

Interestingly, math and music theory are in many ways simpler to understand than the humanities a good number of us instead gravitate toward. Unlike philosophy, sociology, and psychology, for example, music and math are closed systems, meaning that they contain a finite set of logical rules that, once comprehended, become easy to work and even to play with.

The reason it doesn't seem this way, as Einstein pointed out, often has less to do with their inherent complexity, and more to do with how these topics were explained to us in the first place.

Why Singers Need to Know About Technology

The technology of music is another area that singers often steer clear of. All of that unfamiliar software and equipment, all of those complicated concepts that have nothing to do with the art of performing . . . why bother?

In spite of how irrelevant or intimidating it may seem, technology itself isn't difficult to understand. Like math, it mainly appears that way because of how we perceive or have experienced it in the past.

This is great news, as today, musical ability is no longer just a function of how well you can sing, write, and perform. It also matters whether you can properly interact with the technological variables in recording and performance, which is precisely what we'll be talking about in this section:

- What is the process of recording and what do I need to know before heading into the studio?

- How do I properly use a microphone onstage and in the studio, much less pick the right one?
- What do stacking, overdubbing, and comping mean and what other technical terms and concepts are important to understand?
- What are EQ and compression and how do they affect my ability to hear and perform?
- Is it possible to sing with headphones and monitors in a way that sounds and feels natural?
- What do I do when I can't hear myself during a soundcheck and it's just not cool to ask the sound engineer—again—to turn me up? Or worse, when I can't hear myself in the middle of a show?
- What is touring like? What are the rules and protocols of being on the road?

Entering into the professional performance realm without the answers to these and similar questions is a bit like having resisted learning to drive when the car began to replace the horse and buggy. We're not going back, only forward. And to avoid or turn a blind eye to changes in the industry that are coming faster and faster—to think that you don't need to deal with them—can be a career-breaking mistake.

Process, Equipment, Tools, and Concepts

One challenge in talking about technology is that we're all coming to the table with different amounts of experience and knowledge. Like our discussion of vocal technique in *The Art of Singing*, for some people the information here will be entirely new. For others, it may be a bit, if not very, familiar.

I've therefore done my best to provide level-specific layers throughout the section. While we'll cover the basics of the equipment, tools, and concepts for those of you new to the industry or the technical aspects of it, I'll also discuss useful vocal practices as well as often overlooked or forgotten information that will help you, whatever your specific genre or level of expertise.

I'll also go through a number of "other tools" that are rarely discussed in music classes and degree programs—the behind the scenes goings-on of the music business and the lessons that too many of us had to discover on our own, and often the hard way. With any luck, this section will save you time and energy, as well as remind you that you're not alone on this journey. Your concerns and fears, your frustrating experiences and amazing triumphs . . . we've all been or are going there.

Expanding Your Experience

Just as information is power, access breeds familiarity. I therefore want to throw out one last suggestion before we begin about a practice I've found to be tremendously helpful in my own career: stepping into the shoes of your colleagues.

We've already begun this process by exploring the various ways performers and technicians approach their work and one another onstage and in the studio. And this information is invaluable; understanding how other people think and see the world helps us to better relate to and partner with them. There are countless singer- and technician-directed books, blogs, and magazines that will help you delve even further into one another's worlds if you'd like, which I wholeheartedly recommend.

That said, nothing compares with *experiencing* what it's like to be in someone else's shoes. Taking classes, attending workshops, and going to events about recording or singing . . . even working one-on-one with someone . . . will give you—performers and technicians, respectively—hands-on knowledge and experiences that will broaden your perspective, expand your appreciation, and enhance your ability to communicate in ways that nothing else will. Trust me, everyone I know who has gone above and beyond in this way swears that it's one of the best moves they've ever made.

Pre-Production

Unlike technology, which changes almost faster than I can finish typing a page of this book, the processes that guide recording and live performance have remained relatively firm over the years. The space and setup specifics may vary from studio to studio and from venue to venue, yet both involve steps we can look at and learn about.

In the case of recording, these steps are *pre-production*, *production*, and *post-production*. And while they do speak to the before, during, and after of the studio process, they involve far more than that. In fact, pre- and post-production are so integral to the success of a project that even the highest quality recordings can have very little impact when they're not handled properly.

What exactly then is pre-production, and what does it involve? Why is it so important?

In a nutshell, pre-production deals with everything that happens before—and for the most part *long* before—artists and technicians meet in the studio. One aspect of this process, as we've discussed, is establishing who will be on your team. Which producer do you want to work with? What recording engineers do you and he know and trust? Which musicians do you want to play on your record? Is there a certain space where you and they feel most comfortable?

Picking the right people, players, and studio is important, and we'll talk about how to do so at the end of this chapter. Prior to that, however, there are a host of other issues to tackle that will make their selection and the process of recording much smoother and more effective. To say nothing of the amount of time, energy, and money you'll save by doing your homework, which begins by knowing what you want to accomplish.

Clarifying Your Objectives

So often, artists skip this step and run straight into the recording process. Knowing that they need a product to shop to managers, booking agents, radio stations, music supervisors, record labels, or whomever, they're understandably eager to get something on tape that shows off their talent.

The problem is, talent is not necessarily what the industry side of the market is looking and listening for any longer, at least not in a vacuum. While A&R (artists and repertoire) departments at record labels used to nurture and develop unknown singers, today artists are expected to do the majority if not all of the work themselves. Meaning that you need a product that features your voice and artistry in a very specific and polished way, even from the beginning of your career and often from your very first demo.

There are still some labels, managers, and producers out there, along with companies behind televised talent shows like *American Idol*, who are willing to invest the time and resources into a new, undeveloped artist. These men and women might respond favorably to a rough recording of your favorite cover song if both it and you are truly magical.

Yet by and large, this is no longer the case. The music industry has changed and executives have grown accustomed to singers coming to the table with a fantastic demo (as well as a distinctive artist angle or niche, a great live show, and an established fan base). And today, that demo by and large must have the following if you want to gain the interest and support of industry power brokers:

- Exceptional (hit) songs
- A unique sound along with the radio-ready production to match it
- A technical team that can capture both, along with your best vocal

Selecting the Songs

Once upon a time, singers and songs were seen as largely independent entities. Managers, music producers, and A&R departments spent a great deal of time looking for both, hoping to find the perfect material for the artists signed to their rosters.

That match has always been essential; a great melody and lyric, when combined with a meaningful and moving delivery, touches the hearts, minds, and imaginations of listeners. When we think of the top songs and voices of all time, they are rarely one without the other.

For decades, those writing the songs were different from those who sang them in the majority of musical genres. While today many commercial artists write their own material, classical, musical theater, jazz, and country music still find many singers and writers focused on their respective crafts (though self- or cowritten songs are becoming more popular, particularly in country music).[2]

The emphasis today is still on the importance of matching songs and singers, regardless of who writes them. However, there has been a shift—particularly in commercial music—in *when* the two come together, as well as *how* this union comes about.

As we touched upon moments ago, current changes in the marketplace have required singers to be significantly more prepared than their vocal predecessors, including being able to walk in the door with the songs they plan to use commercially already in place. Meaning that most singers need to find the songs themselves.

This has caused a ripple effect not only in terms of who ends up writing the songs for these newer singers, but as well, who ultimately becomes successful as artists. Without connections to established songwriters and publishing companies, vocalists are left to either try their hand at writing or cowriting, or to look for songs from other rising writers and musicians.[3] Those who have access to well-known writers may still find themselves just out of reach of the best material, as they're competing with already established acts with whom all writers hope to place their songs.

Given the competition for fantastic material, it's not surprising that singers who are also great songwriters are getting ahead in today's commercial music marketplace. For example, in *Rolling Stone*'s most recent "Top 10 Artists of All Time" survey (which actually only covers the last fifty or so years), every performer on the list is also the writer of their songs.[4] Even the magazine's top 100 and 500 artists lists feature significantly more singer/songwriters than singers, save for those from the time when labels, producers, and managers scouted material, including Diana Ross and the Supremes, Elvis Presley, Aretha Franklin, and the like.

What do these changes mean for you in terms of practical advice? That from the very beginning of your career as a singer, even while training and preparing for one, you cannot underestimate the importance of original material. Whether you write or not, creating or finding great songs *must* be a priority for you.

This is true regardless of your genre. Even those of you involved in musical theater, jazz, and classical music need to be on the lookout for material that presents who you are as an artist in a fresh and unique way. After all, in every type of music, it's not just about whether you're a great singer with great songs, original or otherwise. It's about finding the right songs *for you*.

Finding material, particularly in the commercial world, means becoming familiar with performing rights organizations (PROs) like ASCAP, BMI, and SESAC, which represent songwriters and publishers, and facilitate relationships between their members and artists. Take the time to learn about them and attend events that these and other songwriting groups facilitate. The same goes for any open mic nights, singer/songwriter showcases, and even interviews with songwriters, artists, and authors on the subject. Go to everything; the more people you meet, the more opportunities you will have for making the connections you'll need to secure, develop, and shop your material.

Also consider offering your services as a demo singer to song, jingle, and commercial writers. Even if you don't get paid much at the beginning, it's a great way to have your voice heard by writers and composers, as well as by the clients and executives they're pitching to. This also goes for voice-over work if you have or can develop a knack for it, as the technical side of the musical and spoken recording worlds tend to have a good amount of overlap. Many people have leveraged these types of seemingly "non-artist" opportunities into successful and lucrative performance careers.

"Never hate a song that has sold more than a half a million copies."

—Irving Berlin

To understand what I mean when I say you need to have "great" material, we need to first make a distinction between *hit* songs and *exceptional* songs. Interestingly, this is an area where many songwriters are at a disadvantage, as they tend to get very attached to the songs they write and, as a result, are not always able to distinguish between the two.

We could spend an entire chapter debating what constitutes an exceptional song, as opinions and personal taste vary greatly. Still, the majority of people in the industry would agree that at the very least, "exceptional" speaks to a high level of quality in writing.

When it comes to what makes a hit song, however, there is no debate. It's all about the song's popularity (or potential to become popular).

That's not to say that hit songs can't also be exceptional. Brilliant songwriters have the ability to distill life's most important and meaningful themes to their simplest and most accessible forms. Finding the perfect blend of exceptional and hit, and of novelty and universality, is the goal of most commercial songwriters and artists.

That said, some songwriters and singers tend to write and gravitate toward wonderfully complex (or at another extreme, murky and unclear) material that moves and inspires *them*, without recognizing that it may not necessarily touch the masses in a similar way.

This is fine if your goal is to produce songs without concern for how well or broadly they may be received. If you're interested in commercial success, however, it is critical to gain the objectivity to distinguish what makes for a great *and* accessible song or, at the very least, to have people around you who can.

Determining Your Sound

How a song is produced has long been one of the most important factors in its success. Looking back, Phil Spector's "wall of sound" in the sixties, the saxophone and synthesizers of the eighties, and the increased use of reverb until the late nineties became sonic standards that the majority of commercial artists necessarily utilized. Even in acoustic recordings, the way the instrumentation and voice are recorded and blended together can make an otherwise good song great.

Today, how a song sounds is not only important, it's critical. Thanks in large part to advances in production technology, innovation and imagination find themselves more and more on par, allowing producers to come up with truly unique, signature styles and sounds that not only enhance a song and artist . . . they are often *the key* to making both successful. As a result, these producers are increasingly claiming writing or cowriting credit for their contributions.

This shift, along with the rise in the number of artists writing or cowriting their own material—out of interest or necessity—and the changing tastes of the listening public has meant that classic "lyric and melody" writers (the two elements that technically define song authorship) have become less in demand. Add to that the decline in songwriting income thanks to the rise of free and reduced cost Internet sites, and it's no wonder that many traditional songwriters are unable to continue in their crafts, or at least to do so exclusively.

On the other hand, because many producers are now also receiving songwriting royalties for what previously would have constituted an arrangement credit, they are staying musically and economically viable in an industry where almost everyone is feeling the pinch. In fact, on *Billboard*'s list of the top twenty songwriters from 2000 to present, all are also producers of the songs they've made famous.[5]

Artists too have realized the importance of participating in more than their primary creative category or categories, including the three on the same *Billboard* list. In addition to singing and songwriting, Beyoncé, Taylor Swift, and Rob Thomas also are given production credit for their contributions, as well as the additional royalties that come with it.

What do these trends mean for you as emerging artists and writers? That you have to pay as much attention to the sound of your songs as to their structure . . . not as an afterthought, but as an up-front consideration. Also key is to become familiar with those who are producing in your style of music and to start considering how to get involved in writing and production yourself if you're not already.

Whether you later hire people to produce the material you bring to the table or create it with them, having a finished track that is a reflection of your sound as an artist is imperative. This of course means that it's also critical for you *to know the sound you are going for*! Very often, singers simply "love to sing" and are open to a wide variety of songs and production styles. Others have a sense of what they want to sound like, but lack either the confidence or the conviction to stay focused when different sonic ideas are presented to them.

While being easygoing and versatile are generally good things, when establishing and pitching yourself as an artist they can hinder more than help. If you don't know who you are, neither will industry insiders or the market into which they want to place you.[6] The same goes when working with writers and producers, who will often default to their own preferred style and sound if you don't make your artistic vision clear.

Having a reel of well-produced songs that sound nothing like one another might be interesting. It may even be the fulfillment of your creative expression. Yet these types of projects have a tough time becoming commercially successful. Established artists have more flexibility when it comes to branching out stylistically, yet this growth tends to happen as a gradual career evolution rather than in the midst of one project.

Honing Your Chops

> "We seem to be losing ability as a society to distinguish between the excellent and the successful."
>
> —Anthony Freud, General Manager, Lyric Opera of Chicago[7]

Production has not only altered the types of songs and sounds that are popular today. It has also changed the way we listen to music and, as a result, what audiences now expect from artists. Thanks to technology's ability to perfect pitch, sounds, and even performances, those standards have become incredibly—and even impossibly— high. And while technology is great for helping to correct issues in otherwise fantastic performances, the sad fact is that too many singers have been over-relying on it and, as a result, are less able to deliver a fantastic vocal.

How many artists today could do justice to "Natural Woman," "Fly Me to the Moon," "Through the Fire," or "The Way We Were" . . . without technological help and enhancements? I'm not saying that artists today should sing or sound like Aretha, Frank, Chaka, and Barbra. The problem is that many of them can't.

I'll never forget when I sang backup vocals for Def Leppard at the VH1 Rock Honors in 2006, where Queen, Judas Priest, and Kiss were also being recognized. In addition to performing themselves, four newer rock bands were also there to play in tribute to them.

While everyone did a fine job, there was just no way around the fact that the older bands sounded better than the younger ones. Granted, they'd been around and playing together longer, but that's not why their performances were so much stronger. It's that throughout their careers, they had to deliver day in and day out live and in the studio. Whereas today, technology in both often picks up the slack for the vocal, musical, and even creative weaknesses that used to be resolved by constant practice and the constant need for a full, top performance.

This isn't such an issue in the musical theater and classical realms, where the rigorous demands of performing and the general lack of overproduction in recording mean that singers still need to be at the top of their game. Those looking to make demos and even records in these genres are further in luck, as production is not usually as extravagant or costly as commercial projects. A home studio, a great mic, and an array of symphonic instrumentation samples can get you an incredibly high-quality recording and a gorgeous capturing of a fantastic vocal performance.

Many great singers in the commercial realm also choose a more organic, less technology-laden production. Norah Jones, Adele, and Ray LaMontagne come to mind, all of whom thrive in a world of more produced contemporaries. While they don't shun the technology available to them, their classic and sparse arrangements are refreshing, as is their ability to perform as well live as they do on their recordings.

The moral of the story: don't rely on production to create great vocals. Even though technology can pick up a great amount of slack, that doesn't mean you should count on it to do so. Develop and hone your chops, whatever your genre. You'll be glad you did.

Putting Together the Team

Given the critical nature of sound in most commercial production today, it's interesting how many people wait until they're in the studio to deal with it. I'm amazed at how often artists will proudly share a CD of the guitar or piano-vocal demos they're about to record, having given little thought to the production. When I ask what sound they're going for, they reply that they're "thinking of something like this," or "hoping that it will sound kind of like that."

Even those who do have a good sense of what they want often hire teams that have little to no experience creating in those styles. Instead they're often people the artist knows personally or whose rates they can afford.

Of course finances are an important consideration. Yet paying a little for a demo or record you can't use will often in the long run cost you more than spending a bit more for one that you can. If it's the wrong team for your sound, even when they do a fantastic job, you may very well have to go through the process all over again.

You've got to start by knowing what you want. For your genre and style, do you need signature, radio-ready tracks, or will a live recording of a great band suffice? In either case, what *kinds* of tracks and arrangements? Which instruments, and what *type* of players? Are you willing to have your voice pitched and edited to perfection, or do you want a more natural sound?

Like musicians, producers and engineers specialize in different things. While it's possible to find a team that fulfills all of your musical needs and desires, you may have to prioritize your interests, especially when you're starting out. Not everyone is phenomenal at recording vocals. Not all great voice guys know how to create a good pop or R&B track. Sometimes you may have to go to different people for different things.

Another reason it's critical to think carefully before jumping into recording is that many producers today want a contract and monetary interest in your career in exchange for their services, including partial songwriting credit for their treatment of your songs. This is sometimes true even when you're paying them in a work-for-hire situation.[8]

Contracts aren't inherently bad, nor is sharing songwriting credit when someone contributes something of unique value to your material. That said, giving up creative control and contractual freedom to the wrong people and for the wrong reasons—especially early on in your career—can be frustrating as well as professionally limiting.

To protect yourself, you have to do your homework, which starts with *listening*. Listen to and get to know the producers and engineers of the recordings you love, and listen to those you have access to in order to see if they're similar. Find people who can deliver the goods, ideally for a low and contract-free price, unless their credentials, talents, and connections warrant otherwise.

If you don't have this kind of access, give newer and younger technicians and players a chance. Often they're willing to rehearse and experiment with you on a song or two for little or even no cost. In addition to helping you nurture and develop your sound, you'll build relationships that may last throughout your career.

Of anyone you're considering working with, don't be afraid to ask questions:

- Can you hear artists they've worked with who have a sound similar to yours?
- Can you work on and record one song together for a fee to try things out?
- What is their approach to recording in the studio?
- What are their economic and/or contractual expectations?
- How much time will you be spending on pre-production and recording, and what is the projected timeline from start to completion? (In other words, will you be a priority, or will you be put on hold every time more important or higher-paying projects come around?)
- Who has the final creative say in terms of songs, edits, and arrangements?
- What are the post-recording expectations of everyone involved? Will they help to shop your project, including sharing it with their connections? Is this a work for hire, or is there an additional charge or contractual expectation if they are able to secure a deal on your behalf?

Once you've chosen your team, additional practical considerations come into play. Don't be afraid to ask about them either:

- Will the musicians the producer wants to use be playing out anytime soon? Can you hear them perform somewhere, or sit in on a recording session to make sure you agree that they are the right fit?
- If tracks are to be used, will you have a say in the final versions?
- Does the negotiated rate cover everything, or are musician's fees and track costs extra? Will you need to deal with unions for those performing on your record, or will the production team handle this?[9]
- Who will take care of creating lead sheets and chord charts of the songs for the band and singers, and arrange rehearsals prior to going into the studio? How many will there be?
- How will the project be recorded? Will the band play together in a live room (which is generally a less time-consuming and costly arrangement), or will everyone be recorded individually? If tracks or track elements are used, will musicians be brought in for overdubs? If so, when? When in the

process will you record your lead as well as background vocals? (In other words, how "finished" a track will you be performing to?)

Establishing Expectations

"It's important for vocalists to understand and express what they want when it comes to working with their recording and production team. For example, one vocalist may know what she's looking for, she just needs to capture her voice. Another vocalist may want to say 'you know, if you have any thoughts, I would love to hear them; I'm really open about how I sing this song.' Yet another might do well to say 'I mainly sing live and sometimes need help on my articulation and working the mic in the studio.' We engineers and producers are always working on mind reading, but as a general rule, we can't. So don't be afraid to tell us the honest truth."

—Jason Garner, Producer/Engineer, Nashville, Tennessee[10]

These questions might seem a bit nitpicky, particularly when just starting a relationship. But trust me, it's so important to ask them. Knowing the who, what, where, and when of your project makes a big difference in your experience of it and, therefore, how you perform on it.

This can be a challenge for many singers who, once they've selected a team, are eager to turn the reins over to them. Sometimes this is due to a great relationship and trust. More often, however, it is because of the singer's own lack of knowledge and experience.

"It's massively important that the producer knows precisely what will be expected of him on a project. Is it my job to just document a song as the artist envisions it? Or does the writer want my creative input and investment to make the song the best it can be? If so, this *must* be discussed before engaging, whether or not I will be included as a cowriter for my efforts. Because it will directly affect my efforts."

—Robert Wright, Producer/Engineer, Nashville, Tennessee[11]

It's time to empower yourself and to speak up. Nothing is more frustrating than when people are trying to do what they think are their jobs, only to find themselves thwarted by unclear expectations. Great producers and engineers can and do wear many hats in the studio; they just need to know which one to put on for your project.

CHAPTER ELEVEN

Production: Hardware and Software, Recording Logistics, and Microphones

The Basics

Today, there are countless ways to go about recording a project, depending on your creative vision and personal preferences. The entire band can play together, everyone can head separately to the studio—or even to different studios—to record their parts, or you can lay down a vocal over a song made up of exclusively computer-generated elements in your bedroom.

This flexibility comes courtesy of music recording software, which since its inception in the 1980s has revolutionized the recording industry. Programs like Pro Tools, Reason, and Logic Pro have made making music infinitely more portable, inexpensive, and user-friendly than it used to be, when producers used magnetic, or analog tape—large reels of film that would have to be literally sliced, reorganized, and pasted back together when edits were needed!

How do the computer and recording software capture and interact with music? First, the live sound has to be converted into a digital format that the software can understand. While we still hear the signals going into the computer and coming out of the speakers as music, what we're hearing has been translated by a piece of external hardware called an *audio interface* into a series of numbers (0s and 1s, to be exact). Called *bits*, these numeric pieces of information are how computers process and store all data . . . whether music files, pictures, or e-mails. With instruments and voices, the computer breaks up and assigns a value to each part of the sound wave, or signal.

I'd wager that most of you are pretty computer savvy when it comes to e-mailing, writing, surfing, and the like. Music software runs on the same platforms and systems and is designed to be just as easy to use. There is a learning curve of course, but the aspects important for artists to understand aren't much more complicated than working with Excel, Word, or Chrome.

When starting a new session, the engineer opens up a new file, just as you would a Word document or an Excel spreadsheet, and records each musical element to a separate track within that file. The voice, through a microphone, goes on one stereo track (right and left), and the guitar—through either a microphone or a cable plugged into the audio interface—another. An entire band could also be recorded to a single track, though usually each instrument is given its own, to simplify organizing and editing.

Thanks to today's software, a song can have anywhere from two to two hundred tracks, depending on how many different sounds, voices, and instruments you want.

Stacked horizontally on the screen, the tracks can be recorded, played, and edited either individually or simultaneously.[1]

Recording a Session

Setting Up the Room

In addition to the software, a host of other tools are involved in the recording process. If you've been in a studio before, you've seen the mammoth mixing console, various computer screens, and racks of hardware lined up against the wall in the control room where the technicians work. Singers and musicians record in separate rooms varying in size from studio to studio, though generally there is a larger live room in addition to a single or multiple smaller isolation booths. Home studios, of course, are set up in more compact and creative ways.

In every studio, rooms are ideally sonically secluded from one another (though generally connected via windows) so that performances can be captured as clean takes. Without sound interference known as "bleed" from other players or ambient noise, it is easier for the engineer to later edit and manipulate the content.[2]

The exception to this rule is in the live room, where players are able to perform together in an organic setting. Plugging in the instruments allows their sound to travel in isolation to different tracks, which the engineer can then work with as easily as if the musicians recorded separately. Singers, drummers, pianists, and other live instrumentalists using microphones can also participate, so long as only one is in the live room; the rest can perform in isolation (or iso) booths adjacent to the space.

Tracking Basics

Let's now look at the experience of recording a vocal—what actually happens when you're in the booth. You'll begin with a soundcheck to establish that your headphone mix is comfortable. Whether or not you can see the engineer, you'll hear him in your headphones courtesy of a *talkback* feature in the control room. Together you'll set whatever balance and blend of your voice and the music you find conducive to your best delivery, while the engineer simultaneously sets the ideal input levels of your voice for the software.

Depending on what point in the project you'll be recording your vocals, you may or may not be singing to a completed track. Often, this decision is based on scheduling specifics out of your control. Over time, you'll learn what kind of arrangement best inspires your performance and can ask to sing to such a track. Better still, through practice you'll develop the skills to generate a fantastic vocal whether or not the instrumentation has been completed.

Even with a final arrangement, your engineer may still want you to sing with a *click track*—a metronomic click set to the bpm (beats per minute) of the song. A click is particularly important when only a few instruments have been recorded, a piece has a sparse arrangement, or when the vocal line begins prior to the music. In addition to keeping you in time, working with a click track is a great way to be certain that the song is the tempo you desire and that everyone is firmly locked into it.

Ironically, click tracks are distracting for many singers, causing them to overly focus on the rhythm and, as a result, to be more out of pocket than they might normally be. If you find this to be the case, as with most things in the studio it just takes practice and some getting used to.

Vocal Editing in Real Time

Some singers still begin a day of recording by performing a song straight through, as they did in the days of analog tape. Barbra Streisand, for example, is known for coming into the studio, doing two top-to-bottom vocals, and then leaving.

Today, however, you'll more likely be a part of the editing process in real time, which involves working on songs section by section. You may be asked to record all of the verses first, followed by the more emotionally and sonically intense bridge and choruses to make things easier for you to conserve energy and the technician to balance levels. Sometimes sections or even the entire song will be recorded line by line.

Just before the engineer punches you in, you'll hear a bit of pre-roll in your headphones—either your previously sung line or, in the case of a new phrase, the music that precedes your vocal. It's always best to sing along with your earlier take and try to match your phrasing and breathing as much as possible to help the final vocal to sound as if it were done in one take.

While you won't be doing the actual editing yourself, you'll be able to see the various audio clips you've recorded and the dead or silent spaces between them displayed on the screen. Your vocal may often be recorded on more than one track, particularly when phrases are too close together to punch into the same track without interfering with the previous lines.

Once the engineer has what he needs for the song or section you're working on, a cursory editing process begins, called putting together a *comp*, or *composite* track. Even when you've done your best to sing the same way throughout the session, some editing is always required to create natural-sounding transitions between the various takes. This includes the use of *fades* at the beginning and end of punched-in phrases (*fade ins* and *fade outs)* and between different takes or regions (*crossfades*).

While the engineer is just as interested in a great final vocal as you are, your intimate knowledge of your own voice means that you'll often hear—or see—the need for edits that might otherwise go unnoticed. So pay close attention. Whether in your headphones or in the control room listening down to a comp, once an engineer is done working on the track, don't hesitate to speak up if something doesn't sound quite right.

After a lead comp is assembled, you'll move on to recording vocal *overdubs*, such as background and stacked vocals (doubling or tripling lines in the lead or background parts to thicken the sound). Often the engineer will "fly" or copy and paste certain lines to future repeated occurrences, such as the lead vocal of a chorus or the stacked background vocals that accompany it, particularly when sonic consistency is desired or there is a time constraint.

Managing Your Mindset

Some engineers wait to do any editing until singers have finished recording, though a certain amount of editing in real time is more the norm, as it lets them assess what they have and need while the singer is still there.

While this approach gives you the chance to focus on and master each specific section and phrase, performing sections of a song out of context and taking frequent breaks to edit often throw singers out of the zone. Not only is it hard to capture the magic that comes from a true performance in this way, staying musically and emotionally connected through numerous stops and starts requires its own kind of stamina as well.

There is also the amount of time the process takes. As we discussed in Section Two, while an engineer can work on a single song for hours, it can be physically challenging for a singer to do so, especially when she needs to nail phrases cold again and again. With practice and experience, this type of work becomes easier, yet for singers new to the studio this tends to be tough.

> "It is extremely difficult for even the most experienced vocalists to have any perspective on their performance while it's happening. For this reason, a producer is the voice of reason and experience who knows how to encourage a vocalist to do one more vocal pass or help them realize that it would be better to take a break and come back to fight another day."
>
> —Cliff Goldmacher, Producer/Engineer[3]

Interestingly, the most difficult aspect of editing in real time is often a psychological one, involving how and when a singer chooses to listen to the various takes she's recorded. Should she hear each line played back in her headphones before moving on and decide whether or not she should try again? Should she periodically head into the control room to listen down to the track? Or should she trust her team to let her know when they have what they need?

For most singers, staying focused on performing is the best choice. Trying to switch back and forth between singing and listening is not only distracting, it also tends to bring out an inner critic that causes more problems than it solves.

Over time, you'll figure out what works best for you. Are you the type of vocalist who is able to sing a song straight through twice, trusting yourself to deliver your best takes as well as the engineer to put together a great comp? Or do you want to be a part of the editing process? If so, can you participate in a way that doesn't interfere with your judgment or your performance?

> "No point in worrying about the notes you've already sung. They have already passed by. There are measures fast approaching in which you can try to do better."
>
> —Eric Rudd, Recording Engineer/Producer and Photographer[4]

Whatever type of singer you are, learning how to surrender control and perfectionism is critical. I remember complaining once to Al Schmitt that I didn't like my vocal on a song he was mixing. He reminded me that every recording is simply a capturing of your voice and self at a specific moment in time. Wise words from a great man and brilliant recording engineer.

Microphones

The Fundamentals

As singers, microphones are our gateway to connection and communication in an amplified world. Yet most of us know so little about them, other than that we need them to record and perform!

Microphones are in a class of what are called *transducers*—devices that convert energy from one form to another. In this case, we're converting acoustical (live) energy from a voice or instrument into electrical energy, which occurs when the sound hits a thin sheath of material in the microphone called a *diaphragm*. The resulting vibrations create the electric current, which in turn becomes the audio signal needed for amplification and recording.

While there are many different kinds of microphones (ribbon, crystal, carbon, fiber optic, and so forth), today in the studio and onstage you'll generally be using either a dynamic or a condenser microphone. The biggest difference between them is that dynamics are self-contained; they don't need an external power source to function, thanks to a magnet and coil of wire that generate the necessary electric current.

Dynamic mics are extremely versatile, durable, and relatively inexpensive. They are the workhorses of the microphone family and, as such, can take an incredible amount of wear and tear—including extreme volumes—making them fantastic live microphones. Many singers find one they like and take it with them wherever they go, including to the studio (the Shure SM58 and AKG's D5 are popular choices).

Instead of a magnet and coil of wire, condenser or capacitor microphones contain two plates of very light, non-electricity-generating material, one of which acts as the diaphragm. As condenser mics require an external power source to function, the subsequent signal tends to be stronger. They're therefore much more sensitive and, as a result, great at capturing the nuance in a voice, making them great choices for recording. What they gain in sensitivity, however, they lose in the ability to endure higher volumes.

Other terms you might hear around the studio refer to microphones' polar patterns, or directionality. Terms like cardioid, figure-8, omnidirectional, and multi all refer to where the microphone picks up its signal. *Omnidirectional* mics, as you might imagine, are designed to or have a setting that enables equivalent recording from each direction, making them ideal for capturing a live band or a group of background singers. *Cardioid* mics, on the other hand, are best for single instrumentalists or vocalists, as they pick up their signal from the front. *Figure-8* microphones are bidirectional, optimal for musicians positioned facing one another (or for interviews), while the multi-setting microphone has a number of positional capabilities.

In case you spaced out when we started talking about transducers, capacitors, and polar patterns, here's a quick and simple review: all microphones have a diaphragm, which, when vibrating, creates a signal. Dynamics are more powerful and harder working, yet less able to pick up subtle vocal distinctions. Condenser microphones are more sensitive to nuance, though they're more fragile and less able to deal with higher volumes. All microphones have a polar pattern, which refers to the directionality of where they receive their signal.

As you might imagine, there are many different condenser and dynamic microphones, varying in price, appearance, and specialization.[5] So much so, that the more you learn, the more you may feel that you've entered into the realm of fine wines or antiques; you can never know too much about the slightest of details, and everyone seems to have a powerful opinion about them.

Hearing people speak with reverence about how certain microphones "roll off on the top" or "shine in the middle" is common . . . and true. By design, each has its own sweet spot when it comes to the instruments and voice types it best captures, explaining why this science has become such an art.

Still, microphones don't operate in a vacuum. Like a race car that performs only as well as the person behind the wheel, a microphone often sounds only as good as the singer and engineer recording with it.

While highly skilled engineers can make an average microphone or one geared for a different voice type sound like the perfect fit, certain mics are optimal and even made for specific voices and instruments. For example, AKG's 414 tends toward the "darker" side, while Shure's KSM 44 provides a bit of extra brightness. The Neumann U87 is considered by many to be a fantastic vocal microphone, good on just about any voice, while Shure's SM58 is a particularly great fit for rock voices (as dynamic microphones often are).

You don't have to have tried every microphone in the world or own your own collection of high-end, handmade pieces to capture stunning vocals. What you do need, however, is an objective knowledge about the timbre, quality, and performance style of your own voice, as well as an interest in which microphones or types of mics may be a good fit for you.

That said, even the most knowledgeable singers rarely walk into the studio and choose their own microphones. Technicians generally have things set up before the singer arrives and might take offense at a request for a specific microphone before the session has even started. Particularly considering that the mic is only one piece in the vocal chain—the various pieces of gear, including preamps and compressors, EQ, and the like—each of which leave an equally important mark on the sound of the voice being recorded.[6]

Still, having as much information and experience as possible will prepare you to participate in a conversation if things aren't going the way you and your team want them to go. If you're certain that a specific microphone has captured your vocal beautifully in the past, don't be afraid to share that information. Even if the studio doesn't have that particular model, they may have a similar one that can do justice to your voice. At the very least, the information might help your team to better understand why they're not getting your best sound with their current mic choice.

Using the Microphone

"When you step up to the microphone, your only task is to remember that these songs move you and to sing them that way. Stay away from any and all technical concerns such as whether you're hitting the notes exactly on key or whether your timing is good. All of this can be addressed when you sit back down in the control room to listen to what you've done."

—Cliff Goldmacher, Producer/Engineer[7]

When it comes to your actual singing, what Cliff says is so true. The time for practice and preparation is before you step into the studio. While recording, your job is to be wholly focused on your performance.

That said, there are some technicalities you will need to deal with just prior to and during the session, including the position of the microphone. Its distance from you depends on a variety of factors including the type of mic, the studio, the kind of singing you're doing, your voice, and the engineer's approach. In other words, the "optimal distance" can have quite a bit of range to it, though most singers stand anywhere from one to five inches from the capsule.

Positioned between you and the microphone will be a *pop filter*—a thin mesh or metal screen that filters out many of the pops, clicks, and S's that can cause distortion and peaks in the signal. Some microphones have internal pop filters (particularly dynamic mics), though the majority of those in the studio require an external one.

Sometimes certain words or ways of stylizing overload the microphone's signal even when the pop filter is in place. In these instances, a few tricks will save you time as well as your and your engineers' ears. Turning away from the microphone a few degrees so that your voice is traveling at a slight angle helps to minimize the full force of any highly explosive diction. Holding your index finger just off your lips in the "shhh" position while singing directly into the microphone also decreases the level of signal reaching the capsule by somewhat diffusing the airflow.

Finally, you want both the microphone and the pop screen to be on level with, or even a bit below, your mouth. While the microphone will generally be directly in front of you, it's common for pop screens to be a bit elevated. The higher placement of either—even when it's a tiny amount—can cause you to physically and energetically lift, resulting in tension and fatigue. Discuss this with your engineer and see whether he's willing to position both between your mouth and chin. So long as you tilt your head just the slightest bit downward while singing, there shouldn't be a problem.

In terms of your performance, you may be asked to sing as you normally would, with the engineer and gear accommodating for the variances in your voice. Or you might have to "work the mic" a bit, adjusting your delivery and distance from the capsule somewhat to help balance out the input signal.

While working the mic is more common in live performance, every song and singer is different—as is every microphone and vocal chain. A great technician should be able to set the levels to allow you to deliver as natural a performance with as little extra thought and movement as possible, though some singer-side adjustment is occasionally needed to help the recording process.

Space and Proximity

"The tape doesn't lie."
—Mark Casstevens, Multi-instrumentalist specializing in acoustic guitar[8]

For many singers, the studio shines a light on habits we haven't noticed before. In addition to hearing what we *really* sound like—perhaps for the first time—we're also made aware of certain physical habits that get in the way of our studio as well as our live expression. For example, vocalists who jerk their heads up at high notes, push too much air, sway from side to side, or use exaggerated diction will hear about it . . . on tape and from their teams.

What's more, the studio characteristics that make it ideal for capturing a great sound aren't necessarily so for creating one. The proximity of the microphone and pop filter can cause even the most experienced of singers to dull, deaden, or bring back the volume of their voices. The same is true of the rooms you'll likely be singing in. Not only are isolation booths sonically dead by design, they also tend to be small, causing many singers to unknowingly modify their delivery to try to fit the space.

Consider the difference between how you would speak to someone six feet away as opposed to someone standing right next to you. It's no different when we're singing in a big open space versus in a tiny room standing an inch away from a big piece of metal (and often with our mouths pressed against the pop screen). Intellectually, we know we're free to sing as loudly as we'd like. Still, for some it takes as much determined thought to sing in full voice into a studio microphone as it would to yell into someone's ear.

It takes practice and a bit of trial and error to learn how to expand rather than contract in these situations. Many singers will close their eyes and imagine themselves in a larger, more natural sonic environment. Others find that focusing on a spot beyond the glass and projecting their energy and voice into that area will help to release both. Moving into the live room, if possible, is always a great idea if your team doesn't mind.

Most singers automatically assume that challenges in the studio have to do with their technique or the headphone mix. If at any point during the recording process you find yourself sounding more dull and quiet than usual (or as a compensation, pushing and straining), step into the live room and try the same troublesome pass. You should know in a matter of moments whether the space is a factor.

Voice Production in the Studio

Over the years I've seen two other unsuspecting issues cause big problems for recording artists. And while we're focusing now on the impact of technology on our voice production, they are both actually overlooked basics of how the voice works.

Use of the Breath

> "Singing isn't something you have to push out; it's something that happens on the interior, at the core, in unison with diction."
>
> —Randall Suarez, Singer/Songwriter, Nashville, Tennessee[9]

Many people think of singing as simply a process of air in, air out. And that to create volume, power, and emotional shape, the more the better.

While air is obviously the key component in singing, increases in volume and intensity don't always require more of it. What they require is a change in the pressurization and support of the air in the body.

As a demonstration, place your hand an inch or so away from your mouth and as naturally as possible, say "good morning." Then, say it louder.

Instead of a difference in the amount of air coming out, you'll notice that a shift in the intensity of your support's engagement is what allowed you to raise the phrase's volume. The same is true when we want to alter the strength or shape of our expression. Try saying "how are you?" quietly, then playfully, then with frustration. Again, the amount of exhaled air remains relatively consistent; it's our support mechanism that is doing the bulk of the work.

> "I don't know how else to explain it: BECOME your song. Whatever it is that you're singing, inhabit it fully. Its beat becomes your pulse, its syncopation the movement of your arms and legs, its melody your breath. Sink your consciousness down into it, become it. Then it will tell you how it wants to go. Then you will move in the ways that it wants to. Yes, this is all figurative, but that doesn't make it any less real or true."
>
> —Amado Ohland, Vocalist/Composer, Blacksburg, Virginia

Interestingly, while our speaking voices automatically regulate volume and intensity, it's very common for singers to overuse or inefficiently use air in an effort to do the same. I remember struggling with this issue while training classically in college, as well as the tension that often came with it.

The problem, I now realize, is that I had begun to interfere with the way my voice naturally functioned. Rather than allow my voice to engage first, *then* consider what might need to be adjusted—as I had prior to my training—my intellectual efforts to implement technique, placement, and diction hindered the commitment necessary for my voice, and air, to work optimally. The same thing happens when fear and perfectionism are present.

In the studio, this issue can be further compounded by the microphone. The presence of an object that is designed to capture your performance makes many people try even harder to direct their *air* into the capsule, rather than allow it to record their *voice*. Common instructions by technicians to use a breathier tone, to focus their vocals, and to sing through the microphone tend to reinforce this tendency.

These types of requests can be helpful so long as you remember that they're not literal commands. They're suggestions meant to help you better shape your delivery and sound, which always has less to do with more air coming out of your mouth, and more to do with using the proper commitment and approach.

If you struggle with this issue, do your best to clear it up before you go into the studio. Sing through songs you're comfortable and successful with and observe how your body naturally creates the distinctions of volume and expression. This awareness, along with some practice, should help keep the presence of the microphone from throwing you off.

Directionality of the Voice

Contrary to what the position of the mic might suggest, sound doesn't only travel forward. For that matter, it doesn't come exclusively out of the mouth, either.

These statements often leave people scratching their heads; we sing and speak using our mouths, after all. Where else could our voices be coming from, and in what other direction might they be going?

Let's use another demonstration to answer these questions. Sing through the first couple of lines of a song you like. Then begin the phrases again, this time with your mouth closed (or if you prefer, sing them on an *ng* sound, as in the final sound of the word *sung*).

You'll notice that in spite of your mouth being closed, you're able to create the same notes, and even maintain the phrasing and emotional shaping. The only difference is that now, the air—and still, not a lot of it—is leaving through your nose (pinch it shut if you want to make sure).

Air not only escapes from the mouth and nose when we sing; it also travels to and "dances" in different areas of our bodies, resonating in the head, mouth, chest, and nose. If you didn't feel this a moment ago, try a more rangy song—"Misty" and "Over the Rainbow" are two I like to help experience these sensations.[10]

Without this resonance, our voices would sound entirely different, and not at all beautiful. And while totally cutting off resonance isn't possible, overly focusing on our mouths when singing tends to result in closing the nasal cavity, unattractive diction and artificial articulation, and a disconnection from the body's full support mechanism, which diminishes resonance and leads to pushing and throat tension.

In the studio, the presence of the microphone exacerbates these tendencies. Just as it causes many singers to push too much air, it also encourages them to focus on getting the voice directly from the mouth into the microphone, limiting the colors and textures—as well as the freedom—that are the cornerstones of a truly beautiful instrument.

There will be times you'll have to adjust your delivery somewhat to achieve the best recording, including interacting more directly with the microphone. Still, you should never have to manipulate the fundamental way that you sing or try to have your song—and the entirety of your expression—come solely out of your mouth.

Those accustomed to performing without handheld microphones, including classical and theater singers, understand that support, resonance, color, and the extension of their voices into the world are holistic and whole-body experiences. If you have trouble relating to these ideas, pay attention to your speaking voice. Without the hyperfocus and manipulation that often accompany singing, see if you can feel your voice's movement throughout your body and how its departure into the world is not mouth and forward only.

Also notice how your throat is far less involved in voice production than you might have previously thought. While your vocal folds are of course located in your throat, it is primarily a passageway through which the voice travels. Overfocusing on it in an effort to sense or direct the voice causes muscles to engage that are as unhelpful as they are unnecessary.

Many of the vocal commands teachers often utilize—focusing into the mask, singing up and over, and rounding out or warming up the tone—speak to the whole-body, multidirectionality experience of singing. And while I don't believe we can actively place the voice according to these commands, I do think they are reflecting an experiential truth about what healthy singing often feels like. The next time you're recording, take this into account.

CHAPTER TWELVE

Headphones, Plug-Ins, and Post-Production

"There is no 'right' when it comes to headphones, as 'right' is only in their absence."

—Anonymous

In addition to getting comfortable with microphones, singing in the studio means that you also have to become adept at singing with headphones. As we've discussed, in rare instances you may work with technicians who will instead let you use small speakers in the sound booth, but in the majority of recording situations, headphones are insisted upon. And rightly so from the technician's perspective: they are the best way to ensure that the voice is being captured cleanly, without any bleed from the track into the microphone.[1]

Like microphones, headphones function thanks to a diaphragm, magnet, and vibratory system. And they too have a range in terms of sonic quality. Some are known to be a bit brighter (Sony's MDR7506s, for example), while others have a more natural, midrange sound (Sennheiser makes some good ones). Over time you'll develop a sense of which phones work best for you, as well as how to work with a variety of different pairs.

As with all recording technology, the design and quality of headphones have grown over the years. Every day it seems, companies come out with an improvement or new model that provides a more natural and lifelike listening experience.

In my mind, one of the greatest innovations to date has been the advent of open-back headphones, which, unlike their closed-back relatives, allow for air and sound transfer into and out of the headset.[2] While this design could help singers a great deal, they're discouraged from using them for precisely what makes them ideal: sound exchange. Instead, open-back models are primarily used by engineers, particularly during mixing, who need an objective and more natural listening experience when setting levels.

Challenges with Headphones

Unnatural Hearing

"You and I can agree that listening/singing through headphones is not how we normally listen to ourselves; it's unnatural, and therefore, it can be the trickiest technical thing to navigate between a singer and engineer/producer."

—Jason Garner, Producer/Engineer, Nashville, Tennessee[3]

When we think of singing, we tend to think only of our voices and our ability to hear them. Rarely do we think of the medium that enables both: air.

Air not only bridges the space between the mouth, nose, and ears; it allows the voice to resonate outside the body. And this sound, this blossoming into the room of volume, resonance, and affect, is in fact what we experience as our voices.

What's more, there is an ongoing, reciprocal exchange between vocal producing and hearing that allows us to keep our voices consistent (and healthy). When we want to make adjustments to our singing, and speaking, it is the sound in and reference of the environment that lets us establish and then correct what we want to improve.

Any singer who has ever overfocused on technique knows what I am talking about. When we ignore the room and go into our heads in an effort to identify a problem and make adjustments, we are more likely to hold our breath and manipulate musculature. Try as we might, it's almost impossible to listen to ourselves "inside of ourselves" in this way.

The same is true in the studio, but even more so. For while the music we're singing to and our recorded vocals may sound perfectly normal in our headphones thanks to technology, *producing* those vocals without the air, space, and reference of the room is a foreign and unnatural experience, particularly for new vocalists.

As we talked about in Chapter Seven, this isn't the case with other musicians, as their instruments aren't housed within their bodies. While they may also prefer the reference of the room, their production—the way they choose to play—isn't affected by the lack of space. Unlike many singers, most can set aside the variables of headphones and even a bad mix and play naturally.[4]

Inaccurate Hearing

"Everyone's hearing is very much like a fingerprint. It is unique to the individual, so the way you hear an earphone or a headphone is very different than the way I hear it based on the inner structure of our ears."

—Matt Engstrom, Shure Incorporated[5]

Headphones do more than affect how we hear and sing. They can also alter *what* we hear. Removing one headphone or shifting both slightly off the ears can result in subtle or even dramatic changes to the sound of the music and voice. This includes, for some people, the song going up or down in tune!

Obviously, tracks don't spontaneously modulate. The problem is that we hear differently with one ear than we do with two, and for many of us, our ears are often slightly different in their hearing capabilities—a fact that we usually don't realize until we're forced to listen with one at a time. Like our eyes, though slightly different from each other in strength and focus, together our ears also tend to balance each other out and present a clearer view.

Removing a headphone may give you more of a room reference. Yet the tradeoff isn't necessarily worth it unless you're certain that your headphone ear is healthy and that you can sing well listening to two somewhat different aural experiences.[6]

Even with both headphones on—and two perfectly functioning ears—you still may find yourself listening to an inaccurate representation of the music and your voice. In addition to issues with the mix, hearing damage, illness, congestion, allergies, dehydration, hormonal fluctuations, stress, chiropractic adjustments and a host of other physical factors result in changes in our hearing all of the time. These issues generally go unnoticed in our lives and live performances, as the room's perspective diffuses their impact and helps us to compensate. In the studio, however, this isn't the case.

Working with Plug-Ins

Thankfully, technology has resolved many of these headphone-related hearing issues through the use of plug-ins—software and hardware add-ons that provide specific effects that help to make the music and our voices sound more natural. While there are countless plug-ins for every instrument and aspect of the recording and mixing processes, we're going to talk about those most prevalent in voice recording, which you will certainly run into.

A quick reminder that your headphone mix of a song is separate from the engineer's working mix. In fact, all performers are able to set their own levels as they see fit, even if what they want to hear doesn't constitute a "good mix." For example, you may want more drums and less piano in your headphones, but that doesn't mean that the engineer or any of the other musicians also have to hear those adjustments.

The same is true for plug-ins. If you ask for more reverb or less compression on your voice, those changes don't automatically transfer to the working mix. Similarly, during the mixing process the engineer will employ a series of plug-ins to polish your final vocal performance and the track, even if you were listening to an unaffected, raw version of both during recording.

EQ

> "Equalization is one of the most powerful tools in your sonic toolkit and can be your greatest enemy or your greatest ally in the battle for the perfect sound."
> —David Mellor, *Sound on Sound* magazine[7]

EQ, or equalization, is the boosting or cutting of certain frequencies to achieve a desired tonality.

What does this mean exactly? At its most basic, all sounds are made up of frequencies, the levels of which can be adjusted to make them more natural-sounding for the recording or performing singer and pleasing to an audience. The low, mid, and high frequencies of each sound can also be tweaked and "moved" a bit, so that competing instruments (those in the same or a similar frequency range) don't lie on top of and conflict with one another, making it easier for singers and musicians to hear themselves and one another clearly.

To better understand how EQ relates to our voices, let's take a closer look at what we mean exactly by frequency. When a note is generated, it affects the surrounding air pressure. These fluctuations or oscillations in air pressure are called the sound's *fundamental frequency*, which is measured in Hertz (Hz).

Every note is defined by its fundamental frequency. For example, middle C on a piano is 261.6 Hz, meaning that the note is cycling 261.6 times per second. The A above middle C—whether sung or played on an instrument—has a fundamental frequency of 440Hz. The higher the note, the faster the cycling, the greater the Hz. (We touched upon this concept earlier when we talked about the futility of trying to create or confirm pitches with your throat; how can you have any direct muscle control over two tiny flaps of skin moving hundreds of times a second?)

In addition to each note's fundamental frequency, other frequencies are also present. Called *harmonics, partials,* and *overtones*, these frequencies are vibrating at various regular and irregular intervals above the fundamental frequency, or pitch. For example, when an A above middle C (440Hz) is sung or played, 880Hz is one of the harmonics present. Whichever overtones are perceived and emphasized, naturally or through EQing, results in the instrument or voice's unique sound, tone, and color, also known as its timbre.

In addition to helping to bring out someone's natural timbre, EQ is also used to help make changes to a singer's voice production during the recording process by highlighting and downplaying certain frequencies. For example, if a singer tends to be a bit strident, exaggerating the high end of her voice will often coax her into warming up her tone.

Unfortunately, an incorrectly EQed vocal can cause a singer to manipulate her sound in undesired and unpleasant ways, usually without her knowing it. What's more, when specific frequencies are overly limited, the voice's fundamental pitch can seem to disappear, leaving the singer unsure of whether or not she is in tune. Similarly, overly boosting certain frequencies can alter a singer's perception of the pitch of her voice and instruments, causing her to be off.

Again, these issues are exacerbated when it comes headphones, as the lack of air and perspective of the room prevent us from being able to recognize the difference between natural and manipulated fundamental and overtone frequencies. Headphones make our listening experience literal as it were, which we react to literally. In an acoustic setting, we wouldn't shift our pitch or voice production if the music or our vocal had too much high or low end on it. With headphones, however, we often can't help it.

It can be maddening to hear yourself and the music perfectly in tune in your headphones, only to go into the control room to realize that you were a half tone off for the entire take. Or more, to hear yourself warbling all over the place, having unconsciously searched for a pitch your ears simply couldn't distinguish.

When these types of wild swings in your vocal performance (and seeming vocal ability!) occur, there is a good chance that EQ issues are in play. If so, a great first step is to request to have all of the EQ removed from your voice and possibly the other instruments in your headphone mix. In the event you're still having trouble hearing well or sounding normal—perhaps because certain instruments' frequencies are competing with those of your vocal—a bit of *panning*, which we'll discuss in a moment, should help to create the space you need to gain a proper perspective and perform well.

Compression and Limiting

As we touched upon in *The Art of Singing*, compression is the use of an electronic device to reduce the dynamic range of a signal by either raising or lowering its volume level.

Said another way, compressors make sure that the loud parts don't get too loud and that the soft parts don't get too quiet.

While it might seem counterintuitive given the name, the main purpose of compression is actually to make things louder. Rather than turning down a track's overall volume to accommodate its loudest spikes, reducing the levels of those spikes allows for the level of the entire track to be raised. This makes for a more even and enjoyable listening experience and, as we'll discover in our discussion of mastering, a more powerful-sounding record.

Limiting, in essence, is an extreme form of compression, used primarily as a protection mechanism for the equipment. Unlike a compressor, which works to contain signal levels within a specific dynamic range, a limiter has a hard stop or ceiling that cannot be passed. When a vocal or instrument goes above the limiter's setting and threatens to overwhelm the signal, the sound snaps back to the threshold established as the loudest acceptable level. A compressor tends to be much more gentle and, if used correctly, inaudible to the performer and listener.[8]

Compression is critical when it comes to amplified sound. Not only does it maintain the integrity of a recording by preventing distortion and wild swings in volume, it also protects aural health. After all, a live vocal can only be so loud; you'd have a tough time blowing out your own ears singing in a normal room. Amplification, however, throws natural law out the window by allowing for any amount of signal to be funneled directly into your ears, which is why a protection mechanism needs to be in place. Without the proper use of compression and limiting, amplified sound can (and often does) cause hearing damage, both in performers and members of the audience.

On the other end of the dynamic spectrum, compression also allows us to hear vocal nuance in quieter singing, which might otherwise be lost when competing with instruments in a recorded track. In these instances, compression removes the tendency of a vocalist to push by lifting quieter vocal passages, as well as bringing down very loud ones, so that the entire vocal sits just on top of the instrumentation.

In this way, like EQ, compression has the ability to improve a vocal performance. Rather than concern yourself with hearing and volume regulation, when used expertly, compression encourages you to sing with abandon. Both heartbreaking subtlety and gut-wrenching power sound perfectly in the pocket, just as they would on your best live day. And sometimes even more so.

In spite of the many benefits, compression can also create problems. Whereas EQ often causes issues with pitch, compression tends to result in tension when three factors are incorrectly managed: when the compressor kicks in, how much compression is used, and the way that it engages.

Again, the job of vocal compression is to place the voice just above the music so that it can always be heard by the singer and listener, regardless of the dynamics of her performance. This sweet spot is known as the *target range*, which the compressor works to maintain by raising the level of anything that falls below it, while turning down anything above it.

However, if the range isn't set correctly, certain parts of the vocal won't be heard or will be too loud. Let's say for example that the target range is 75 to 85 percent for the voice to sit correctly in the mix. If the range is set below that, the quieter parts of the vocal disappear into the track, causing many singers to either go off pitch or to push in an effort to hear themselves. Conversely, when the range is set too high, the louder parts become far too loud, leading singers to pull back on their energy.

The second issue is how much compression is used within that target range; in other words, the amount your vocal is reduced or increased when the compressor kicks in. Typical ratios for vocals are 1.5:1 where dynamics are reduced by about a third, or 2:1 where they're reduced by half. Set any higher than this and even subtle changes in vocal volume are dramatically exaggerated, causing singers to hesitate. Improper ratio settings can also cause you to push; when we give a line everything we've got but don't hear that increase in volume in our headphones, singers often—and unconsciously—go overboard, sometimes pushing to the point of strain.

Finally, there is the matter of how the compression engages, involving what are called *timing parameters*. Engineer Robert Wright uses a great analogy of a car radio to explain the concept: Imagine that when you first turn the radio on, it's far too loud. The amount of your initial, reactionary adjustment is called the *attack parameter*, and the amount you then bring the level back up so it sits in an ideal range is termed the *release parameter*. Compression works the same way, with the attack and release parameters dictating how we experience compression engaging and adjusting.

Let's look at an example to bring the whole concept of compression home. When your vocal is out of the established target range (75 to 85 percent, for instance), the compressor will either reduce or boost your level to bring it back into range. Assuming that the ratio (the amount of compression being used) is approximately 2:1 or 1.5:1, and that the attack and release parameters are set appropriately, you shouldn't notice anything other than a natural-sounding increase or decrease in your volume. If something does sound off, this information will hopefully help you to better understand and communicate about it when the issue arises.

Reverb and Delay

"Reverb, or echo, is very useful and important, especially when talking about the voice. It's what gives space around the various instruments, and especially the voice, for creating depth and dimension."

—Bill Schnee, Grammy and Emmy Award–Winning
Producer/Engineer, Los Angeles[9]

Reverb, or reverberation, is the sound that continues on in the room after the source of that sound has stopped. If you've ever sung in a concrete stairwell or in the shower, you know what reverb is . . . it's that glorious echo that makes us all sound like superstars. As a matter of fact, the first reverb used on a record was created and captured in a bathroom.[10]

Those new to recording occasionally confuse reverb with *delay*, which is a true echo—the deliberately spaced out repetition of a word or phrase, which diminishes in volume over time. The effect is generally added during the mixing process, as performing with a delay can be terribly distracting. Anyone who has ever sung in an arena knows what I am talking about; I'll never forget my first time, being shocked and distracted by that "other singer" who kept repeating my lines!

As Bill points out, reverb rounds out the sound of the voice, giving it life and body in a recording. And while it isn't as popular today as it was in the 1980s when records were drenched in it, most singers still use at least some reverb in their headphones, even when their final vocal is utterly dry. It brings the critical space and room element we've been talking about to the headphone mix, allowing vocalists to hear themselves more naturally and, as a result, to sing well.

That said, reverb sometimes has the opposite effect. The wonderful sound of reverb can give us the illusion that our voices sound better than they do (hello, bathroom and stairwell!) making us lazy in our energy and engagement. Lowering the amount of vocal reverb usually solves the problem when we start sounding dull and lifeless in the control room, if not in our headphones.

Another issue with reverb is that it is sometimes used to try to fix or gloss over unrelated mix issues. For example, reverb is sometimes added to a poorly EQed or compressed mix in the hopes that the spaciousness will encourage an improvement in the singer's performance. It rarely works, as we discovered with Nancy in Chapter Six; it just makes the already problematic mix sound more murky.

Panning

To understand panning, we first have to take a look at the difference between *mono* and *stereo* sound. Mono, or monophonic sound, as the name implies, comes from a single source. Prior to the 1940s, all music and audio was recorded and played back through a single channel.

That changed in the 1960s with the popularization of stereo sound, which uses two or more independent channels for both recording and listening.[11] Sound could now be heard through multiple speakers, allowing for a more lifelike listening experience. Studio headphones, a home audio system, and your iPod's earbuds are modern examples, all of which have a left and right stereo mix.

Panning takes the development of stereo sound a bit further, allowing for the deliberate positioning of certain instruments and voices within a mix. Instead of hearing the same mix in both speakers, the original use of panning made it possible to put certain instruments and voices exclusively on the left and others on the right. (The Beatles' stereo versions of the albums *Rubber Soul* (1965) and *Abbey Road* (1969) are examples.)

This "hard panning" is rarely used today, as it's not particularly natural sounding. Instead, engineers now have the ability to sonically place the instruments and voices at various points along the left-right continuum. If you imagine a clock, the piano might be positioned at ten, the guitar at two, and the voice, bass, and drums somewhere around noon, similar to where they might be located in a live show. When the instruments and voices are placed where our attention will best focus on them, and those that share the same or similar frequencies are separated out, recordings are more natural sounding and impactful.

Panning is just as important in the recording process as it is in a final mix. As we discussed in the EQ section, certain instruments can blend and overlap with the voice, making it difficult for a vocalist to hear herself in her headphones. Rather than EQ each instrument to manufacture space, panning can more easily alleviate the problem.

This is a must when recording background vocals, particularly if you're doing your own. If instruments with similar timbres are hard to hear, imagine how difficult singing along with yourself can be, especially when you're stacking vocals. By panning the recorded vocals to one side and your live vocal to the other, the aural confusion melts away.

Interestingly, some singers find that hearing their voices more predominantly in one headphone causes them to push with the other side of their throat in an effort to balance out the sound. As hard as it might be to conceive of someone straining with only one side of his or her voice, it happens all the time. Unlike a live show, where we can interpret directionality without it affecting our sound, headphones prevent that perspective and our muscles respond accordingly.

Lastly, beware of panning as a cure-all, especially when it's used in conjunction with other plug-ins. A bad sound is a bad sound, regardless of which ear you hear it in; if you're still struggling to hear yourself when the instruments and voices have been properly spaced out, be sure to check whether EQ, compression, and other levels have been set correctly.

Auto-Tune

"The use of Auto-Tune has become out of control. Even great singers are demanding that pitch be corrected to literal perfection. What singers should be more concerned with is telling the story of the song with all the emotion they can to make that story compelling for the listener. It should make them want to hear the next chapter (verse) and the moral of the story (the chorus) again and again."

—Bill Schnee, Grammy and Emmy Award–Winning
Producer/Engineer, Los Angeles[12]

Auto-Tune—as the name implies—is a pitch equalizer. It takes a vocal line (or a line of any melodic instrument) and nudges it into tune anywhere that it is off. You can set the controls to be either loose or stringent, even going so far as to manually graph the desired adjustments down to perfecting each quiver of a vibrato.

Conceptually, Auto-Tune is a great tool. If you deliver a fantastic vocal save for a couple of off notes, Auto-Tune will correct them without your having to punch in those lines and risk the sound and spirit of your delivery not matching up with your original take.

Unfortunately, as Bill points out, Auto-Tune has become overused to the point of madness. It's now common for entire songs to be Auto-Tuned, including passages and notes that are already in tune. Even if you're inclined to want a less produced, more natural sound, many producers won't give you the choice, as audiences have become so accustomed to perfection in recordings that they balk at anything else.[13]

This obsession with pitch has had an impact on what is expected of singers in the studio and, as a result, how we practice and prepare. Many technicians will end a session before an exceptional vocal has been delivered, as one is no longer necessary to create an exceptional recording. No longer needing to nail our vocals, many singers have accepted the notion that "good enough" is indeed good enough, even at the professional level.

This is also the case in live performance, where Auto-Tune is increasingly used on microphones in real time (and even sometimes in the studio). Instead of inspiring artists to work harder, the pitch and performance perfection of their recordings courtesy of Auto-Tune and editing leads many to again lean on technology, rather than try to re-create such impossible standards.

This growing vocal apathy worries me. Not only is it important to develop and maintain our chops for vocal health (and to be the best that we possibly can), we also don't know where listener preferences will lie in the future. Taste swings like a pendulum and, at some point, people will again become interested in the rawness and realness of the human voice. Those who've neglected the basics will find themselves out of practice and possibly out of work.

"I want to be moved, more than anything else, when I'm listening to music."

—Dawn Upshaw[14]

Ironically, Auto-Tune also makes some studio singers anxious . . . and pitchy. The knowledge that their voices are going to be so closely scrutinized and later corrected causes them to overly focus on their notes while performing, resulting in an increase of tension and pitch issues.

To be clear, thinking about pitch isn't a problem; it's impossible to not have it at least somewhat in mind when working on a record. Yet knowing that it is such an issue distracts vocalists from delivering a great performance, compounding the technical variables and career and confidence issues that are already in play in recording.

In the studio and out, keep in mind that correct pitch is never achieved through physical or mental tension, but rather, through the dual processes of *listening* and *allowing*. When you concentrate on hearing the music and melody line correctly and permit your instrument to create the latter, you will rarely go wrong. Focus on that when you're recording, and worry about Auto-Tune and all other editing tools and choices once you've left the booth.

Troubleshooting Plug-In Issues

As helpful as plug-ins are designed to be, things don't always go according to plan. Thankfully, being informed about the technology will help you to recognize issues when they come up so that you can partner with your team to resolve them. This includes taking the following steps during your session:

- **Participate fully**. Soundcheck is like breakfast—the most important meal of the day, yet the one most often skipped. It's critical for ensuring that your levels are set correctly and that you're comfortable with them, so don't fake your way through it. The excitement and adrenaline that kick in when the red light comes on take things up even another notch, making it all the more crucial to treat your soundcheck like your actual performance as much as you can.

- **Pay attention**. In addition to singing full out, pay close attention to what's going on during soundchecks. While you won't get (and don't need) a running commentary of every adjustment the engineer is making, it's important to start developing an awareness of what changes are being made as well as what those changes sound like in your headphones. This way, you're able to help with troubleshooting if and when things don't run smoothly.

- **Communicate**. For many singers, particularly those new to the studio, it's easy to clam up when the first day of recording rolls around. While understandable, fears of being pushy, uninformed, or annoying are nothing compared to the sinking feeling at the end of a session that you could have done a better job. So if you hear (or don't hear) something, say something. Patience is necessary at the front end when levels are being set, of course. But if you're in the swing of things and are struggling to hear yourself, or your voice production feels or sounds unnatural in any way, don't be afraid to speak up.

- **Be flexible**. Even when everything is set perfectly and you're working with an expert, you may still be asked to make some adjustments to your performance. Whether it has to do with your dynamics, style, or vocal coloring, certain voices need a little help to best capture them. Therefore, be prepared to modify your delivery and to do so consciously and without affecting your artistry. Just like mic technique, the ability to make vocal modifications while retaining interpretation is a skill. The sooner you start practicing, the better.
- **Keep an open mind**. Once in a while you may be asked to do things that don't seem to make sense. Be willing to set your doubt aside when those you trust are requesting a change of gears. Remember, your team has a greater amount of perspective in the control room than you do in the recording booth. Listen to what they have to say and try it on with an open mind. More often than not, you'll be amazed at how well even seemingly out-of-the-blue suggestions will work. If they don't, you didn't lose anything by trying.

Translation Guide for Singers

"The goal of a good relationship onstage and in the studio is creating an effective language with sets of references so that singers, engineers, and producers can communicate effectively."

—Robert Wright, Producer/Engineer, Nashville, Tennessee[15]

Even when you take these steps, resolving hearing issues can still be a challenge given the experiential divide that exists between singers and technicians. Throw into the mix how difficultly we communicate and it's no wonder how a singer's perfectly lucid account of her experience might mean nothing to an engineer, and a clear explanation of his technical choices may seem to fall on deaf ears.

My friend Robert Wright—an incredibly intuitive and talented producer/engineer—and I therefore put our heads together to come up with a "translation guide" for some of the most common issues singers encounter in vocal recording (as well as in live sound), many of which involve the plug-ins we've just been discussing. We hope it will provide a good reference as you start to gather your own explanations for how your experiences translate into technical terms.

To that end, I recommend taking some notes the next time you're in the studio. If something seems "muddy" to you, ask the engineer what the problem is in technical terms, as well as what he'll do to fix it. You don't need to know exactly what frequencies he'll be boosting or cutting, or how much he'll adjust the gain or timing parameters unless you're ready to communicate at that level. Just understanding whether the problem is EQ- or compression-related will be tremendously helpful, as will learning what language might best assist your team in understanding and resolving those challenges.

What Singers Say:	What It Means to Engineers:
Muddy	EQ issue: Too much lo-mids (200–300Hz)[16]
Bright	EQ issue: Too much top end (6–10KHz)[17]
Heavy	EQ issue: Too much around 150Hz
Flat	EQ issue: Too lo-fi, needs more top and bottom (8–10KHz, 100–200Hz)
Thin	EQ issue: Not enough lo-mids, too much hi-mids (3–6KHz) or top end
Squeaky	EQ issue: Too much hi, hi-mids (8–12KHz) OR Compression/Gain issue: Mic's about to feed back on the top
Hissy	Compression/Gain issue: Likely that levels are not adjusted well (especially with live wireless systems) OR EQ issue: Too much very top end (8–12KHz)
Tinny	EQ issue: Combo of too much hi-mids around 4–6KHz AND Compression/Gain issue:[18] A touch of distortion or static in wireless (live) systems
Ugly	Other: Garbled audio from wireless interference, possible digital artifacts in digital wireless (live)systems OR Other: More information needed
Soft	Compression/Gain issue: Not enough level OR EQ issue: Needs more hi-mids
Loud	Compression/Gain issue: Too much level or needs less compression
Aggressive	Compression issue: Too much and too fast (timing parameters) OR Gain: Too loud
Echoey	Reverb issue: Too much reverb/delay
Dark	EQ issue: Too much lo-mids
Cutting out	Short in cable or other connection(s), dead/dying batteries in wireless (live) systems

Again, these are common technical explanations of what many singers experience. "Flat" and "aggressive" won't always mean the same thing to you as they do to another vocalist and thus, the importance of keeping your own notes. You may also find yourself reaching for terms that will be entirely your own. I've heard some singers talk about their headphone mix sounding too "blue" or wanting to hear their vocal a little more "purple." As if "muddy," "heavy," and "squeaky" weren't confusing enough!

No one's trying to be difficult. It's just that we're reaching for words to describe sonic experiences we've never had in a live setting and, therefore, have never had to put into words. Fortunately, with practice and a genuine desire to communicate, the experiential-technical divide begins to diminish and even the strangest things we say start to make sense.

A Word of Advice for New Singers

Experience is what allows us to test out and refine our approach in new and unfamiliar situations, as well as ourselves in them. This is certainly the case when it comes to using headphones (and in-ear monitors as we'll explore in the next chapter). It takes time to discover how to hear and sing in such a new way, and for some, it's a career-long process.

The biggest problem for most new singers isn't how long this process takes, it's that they don't realize that it is a process! I can't tell you how many people I work with who are shattered by their early experiences in the studio . . . how they sound, how it feels, and what people have to say about it.

Take Katia, whose engineer on her first project told her that she sounded dead and warbly, even though she'd given it her all and thought she did a pretty good job.

"Maybe it was that I had just gotten over bronchitis. . . ." she wondered. "Or maybe I'm just not as good as I thought I was. . . ."

Self-doubt is by far one of the greatest obstacles singers deal with in the studio. Uncertainty can develop into a full-blown lack of confidence in the blink of an eye, manifesting physically and confirming the singer's worst fears.

Remember that learning to record and perform with amplification is a process. Be humble, be willing to learn, and most of all, be willing to make mistakes. Don't let your first experiences, or what others have to say about them, shake your confidence in yourself or your voice. Get some major, judgment-free practice under your belt before you even begin to assess how you can do a better job. Rome wasn't built in a day; neither was a fantastic recording career.

Post-Production

Post-production, as the name implies, includes everything that happens after the recording process has been completed. And while you'll no longer be involved with the hands-on aspects of it from a performance standpoint, it's good to understand the entirety of the recording process, including what mixing and mastering are and their importance when it comes to an excellent-sounding recording.

Mixing

"Mixing is way more art and soul than science."

—Eddie Kramer, Producer/Engineer[19]

While some editing is done during the tracking process, *mixing* truly begins when the final comps have been delivered to the mix engineer. Technically, the process involves editing, balancing, and polishing each and every track of a song. But mixing is more than that . . . it's the fitting together of each piece of the sonic puzzle so that every element of the song—individually and collectively—shines.

Mastering

"Ninety-five percent of mastering is not in the tools—it's in the ears."
—Craig Anderton, *Sound on Sound* magazine[20]

While many recording engineers also mix records, mixing is a specialty that some dedicate their careers to. The same is true of *mastering* engineers, those who take the final mixes of a record and bring them together and create the product that will go out into the world.

The process of mastering includes putting the songs into their final order, making them sound the same (beyond what the mixing engineer has already done), and finessing their individual and collective levels so that they are equal to one another and as loud as possible (otherwise known as making them "radio ready"). Yet mastering encompasses far more than that. It's the *je ne sais quoi* that either makes a record smack you in the face or barely graze your attention.

Both mastering and mixing have a much greater influence than many realize when it comes to the quality and impact of your record. Make sure that you don't underestimate their importance when establishing your team and setting up the logistics for your next project.

CHAPTER THIRTEEN

Live Sound and Performance

The Studio Versus the Stage

When it comes to technology, there are many similarities between live performance and recording. The microphones and much of the hardware and software are the same, meaning that the plug-ins we just went through are also present in the live arena, along with their benefits and challenges.[1]

The translation guide from the last chapter is also applicable, as the experience of using in-ears and monitors is very similar to studio headphones. And while you'll meet a number of new players in the live setting, including house and monitor engineers, stage managers, and technical, television and touring crews, our conversation about relationships will apply.

Still, there are some significant differences between live performance and recording. Save for stationary, or "sit-down" shows (as in Broadway theaters and opera houses) and longer commercial runs, you'll likely be in a new space almost every day, each with different acoustics and structural dynamics. And unless you're on an established tour and traveling with your own team, you'll also be working with different technicians and crews at each venue.[2]

Particularly in the case of new commercial artists, traveling solo also means that you'll be using some if not all of the house's gear and equipment. Even in the unlikely event that every venue on your calendar has the same rig, there will still be a good deal of variation in sound depending on who's running it.

A new space, a new technical team or team members, new gear, and new settings night after night . . . no wonder performing live can be so challenging!

While these variables are certainly a lot to deal with, it's actually the nature of live performance itself that tends to thwart singers the most. You can work on a record in private to your heart's content, but in performing, you are live from the moment you step onstage until the curtain falls. There is no editing; you can't redo a song or take back a line you don't like.

For some, this is a good thing. The vulnerability and lack of control allows certain singers to surrender and stand confidently and even peacefully in the eye of the storm. Others find that the rush of excitement and adrenaline transforms their nerves into a performance-enhancing force.

Obviously, not all of us are so lucky! Which is why, in addition to learning how to manage the many variables in live performance, we must also learn how to deal with *variables themselves*—how in real time to relax, release, and go with the flow in the face of anything internal or external that comes our way. This is a must, as the one constant in live performance is that something will always be different.

A Look at the Live Arena

Acoustics and Amplification

Acoustics is the science that deals with the production, transmission, and effects of sound. You can't look at the stage or studio without discussing it, though the two require very different treatments. Whereas a dead, reflection-free room is ideal for recording, live performance technicians look to feature and highlight music by optimizing how it travels and resonates within the space. For years, orchestras, opera houses and theater companies relied largely on their buildings' design and sound characteristics to help performers project into and fill their huge spaces. The same is true in many venues today.

Thanks to *amplification*, great sound is no longer dependent on an acoustically perfect setting; a well-designed system can create a fantastic sonic experience in an arena, at an open-air venue, or in someone's basement. Still, factors such as temperature, humidity, the number of people present, and the space's unique characteristics will have an impact on what you hear and, as a result, how you perform. As well, while the stage and the house are traditionally designed to be sonically distinct, there will always be some amount of bleed from the latter into the former whether or not you're using amplification.

The challenge is to learn to stay true to your vocal production while honoring the subtle changes that are often necessary to accommodate whatever space you're in. For those in the classical and theater realms, longer rehearsal periods help singers ensure that they're adequately projecting into the house. Commercial artists with the benefit of amplification but not the luxury of lengthy stays in one venue have to be on their toes and participate fully in each soundcheck.

The Gear

> "More and more equipment is making the move from the recording studio to the stage as its size decreases and its flexibility increases. Perhaps one day all that is achievable in the studio will be achievable onstage. At that point there will be no reason to withhold the label 'studio performance' from 'live' concerts."
>
> —Andrew Kania, "Making Tracks: The Ontology of Rock Music"[3]

To back up Andrew's point, you'll find every plug-in, tool, and piece of hardware we've discussed in the last two chapters in the commercial live arena as well. That also goes for the software. Stand behind any number of live sound guys and you'll find Pro Tools on their computer screens just as you would in the studio.[4] You'll even see the same song files open and running, as many if not the majority of live and televised commercial gigs have at least some portion of the music prerecorded.

There are a number of reasons why this practice has become so popular. For starters, given that there are usually far more tracks on a record than there are members of a band, working with prerecorded tracks helps to deliver a similarly enhanced and "thick" presentation. Having a prerecorded bed of guitars, drums, and background vocals also makes it possible for a few members of a band, or even a single artist, to perform while retaining the record's full impact.

Another reason is that modern audiences have come to expect an artist's live performance to sound similar to if not the same as his or her record. Given the amount of noninstrumental production on many of today's projects, a prerecorded track of these elements is often necessary to deliver what audiences anticipate hearing.

These expectations also apply to vocalists. While full-on lip-synching does still occur, more commonly today singers will sing along with a prerecorded track or tracks of their lead vocal. When the tracked and live takes are mixed correctly, the audience hears a well-delivered, radio-ready performance while allowing the singer a bit of leeway in her delivery. This is particularly important with singers who dance, as their choreography often prevents them from being able to match the quality of their record's vocals.

Of course, not all artists use prerecorded tracks and not all audiences want to hear perfection. Many embrace the opportunity to play and listen to live versions of songs that sound different than their recorded counterparts. This is obviously the case with jazz artists, as well as some in other genres.

Still, while many music consumers claim to loathe lip-synching and singers hiding behind prerecorded tracks, quite a few would be disappointed if they got the authentic performances they say that they desire. It's a bit of a catch-22, with many producers and artists choosing to give fans what they actually want, in spite of the fact that some listeners may not be aware of what that is.

Microphones

The dynamic and condenser microphones we discussed in the recording section are also the most common choices in live performance. Again, dynamics take the lead in popularity onstage thanks to their ability to withstand louder volumes and greater wear and tear. Condensers have their fair share of devotees too, particularly with more nuanced singers and acoustic musicians.

In addition to the handheld mics we also find in the studio, other models are common in the live realm. *Headset microphones*, extending from behind the ear to the mouth (and generally coupled with a monitoring device) are popular with commercial acts and dancers, as their physical stability leaves hands free for expression and choreography. *Lapel* and *lavalier microphones*, located on a singer's clothing or more commonly (and invisibly) along the hairline, are standard in musical theater, where the illusion of a nonperformance reality is critical. Headset, lapel, and lavaliers are also generally dynamic or condenser microphones with built-in windscreens.

Finally, in theater, opera, and other classical performances today, stage microphones positioned either on or above the stage are used to gently amplify performances beyond what the vocalists, musicians, and acoustics of the space do on their own.

In terms of technique, the goal with stage mics, lavaliers, and headsets is to sing as you normally would. Unlike handhelds, there is no "working the mic," as you can't bridge or expand the distance between you and the capsule. Therefore, a proper soundcheck and your consistent vocal delivery are key to ensuring that levels remain in the proper range.

Today, the vast majority of live microphones are wireless. Look at pictures or videos of older bands using handhelds, and you'll see cords running all over the place. Not so any longer. While an improvement in terms of mobility for singers and the safety of everyone onstage, wireless microphones present their own challenges. For starters, they require batteries, which can impair microphone functioning and signal disruption even when they're relatively fresh. As a result, it's common practice to use new batteries at every gig, though smaller venues don't always heed this rule. It's therefore a good idea to bring along some extra or rechargeable double A's to your gigs.

Another issue is that, being wireless devices, each microphone needs to be adjusted to avoid interference with all of the other gear's radio frequency settings. As we saw in the translation guide, hissy, tinny, and ugly sounds aren't always caused by issues with the mix; distortion, static, or interference in the wireless system may also be playing a role.

Perhaps the most common and unpleasant form of interference is *feedback*—the high-pitched screeching that occurs either when the microphone picks up the speaker's signal and cycles it through to the speaker again, or thanks to incorrectly set audio levels. Fortunately, the issue is usually as easy to solve as it is to identify.

Speakers and Monitors

Just as your studio headphone mix and the engineer's working mix are separate in recording, there are also two distinct mixes in live sound. Yet there is nothing "working" about either; whereas the focus in recording is on what the artists need to hear, onstage there are two equally important priorities: what the performers are listening to and what the audience is hearing.

On larger tours and gigs, these needs are met by two systems, each run by their own technician or technical team. The house sound engineer—located in the audience, or house—mixes and delivers the sound through a system of speakers positioned in front of the stage, facing the audience. It is independent from the onstage monitors you'll be using, and as such, is largely out of your awareness.

What you hear is the responsibility of the monitor engineer. Usually located on the side of the stage so that eye contact can be maintained, he is responsible for ensuring that all the musicians hear what they need in their monitor mixes. He may also be in the front of the house, particularly in smaller venues where a single engineer or team is responsible for both the house and stage mixes.

WEDGES

If you're wondering what the difference is between monitors and speakers, the answer is . . . not much. For the most part, the words point to who is doing the listening; speakers direct sound into the audience, while monitors are designed to allow artists to "monitor" the music.

The first monitors came about in the 1960s when amplified sound in the house began to prevent the performers onstage from hearing themselves. To resolve the problem, house speakers were initially placed on the sides of the stage and the music blasted across it. A not entirely effective practice, the speakers were soon moved front and center, where they remain today.[5]

The design of monitors has changed over the years. Today's models, called *wedge monitors*, are much smaller than their predecessors, and direct the music at an angle up toward the musicians. In most cases, everyone has their own wedge, which tend to be very effective in providing accurate, individual mixes in spite of the other stage monitors and ambient noise from the house.

The most important advantage of wedges is that they allow for a natural singing experience. With nothing on or in your ears, you are able to hear a good mix of the music and your voice and, therefore, to sing as you would in a non-amplified setting. That said, differences in performer energy levels between the soundcheck and the show, the quality of the stage and house mixes, and the sound of the audience can alter the onstage sonic experience, making it hard to hear. As well, louder house volumes necessitate louder stage monitor levels, which can lead to sound overwhelm.

IN-EAR MONITORS

Once again, technology solved the problem created by its latest evolution, which in this case came thanks to a man named Jerry Harvey in 1995. A long-time sound engineer for acts including Van Halen, Kiss, Morrissey, Mötley Crüe, and k.d. lang, Harvey created in-ear monitors in response to artists' requests to better and more safely hear themselves than they could with traditional monitors. By eliminating the sound of the house as well as the ambient noise from the other performers and monitors onstage, in-ear monitors allowed artists to hear precisely what they wanted and needed, and, as a result, perform well in any venue and under any sonic circumstances.

After the first successful pair was made for Alex Van Halen, word spread and Harvey started his own companies Ultimate Ears and, later, JH Audio, both of which still provide custom in-ear monitors for artists and musicians around the world today.

In many ways, in-ear monitors are fantastic. I've sung in clubs, on TV, and in arenas where it was almost impossible to hear myself, or anything for that matter, with wedges, in spite of fantastic technical teams. And in-ears would have been a blessing at those national anthem gigs so as not to hear "that other singer" relent-lessly echoing my every word.

In-ear monitors are also excellent for aural health, as they keep the mix volume at a healthy level—even in the loudest of gigs. By extension, this also protects vocal health; no longer straining to hear themselves, the need for singers to push over the band and audience ceases as well.

In spite of the many advantages, in-ears present their share of challenges. In fact, everything we talked about in the headphone section also applies to in-ears, yet to an even greater degree, as headphones at least have a bit of space in and just outside of the ear. With in-ear monitors, whether you have a one-size-fits-all model, or have had a pair custom molded specifically to your ears, they block off all airflow and, thus, all natural perspective. As such, any incorrect sonic presentation causes the body and voice to even more dramatically compensate in an effort to hear a natural sound.

Hearing Through Feeling

"There's no point in getting pissed off when you can't hear yourself. It actually happens a lot. And while it may make things a bit harder, why complain? It's in those moments that I take a second to close my eyes and focus on how the sound *feels* to me. *That* is how I'm able to hear myself when my monitors have failed me. And since you really never know what you're walking into, it's better to learn how to be able to deliver in any and every situation, whether or not 'hearing yourself' is an option."

—Cara Samantha, *American Idol* Contestant, Singer and Songwriter[6]

Of course, some singers have no trouble in the live realm. Whether with wedges or in-ears, they step up to bat, hear what they need, and deliver as usual. The same is true for many in the studio.

Unfortunately, others are not so lucky. Even at the topmost levels of the industry, challenges with hearing are more common than you might think.

I'm not trying to be a downer here and I'm not bashing technology. I'm just pointing out what so many singers have come to accept as part of the reality of singing with tools that can't fully re-create or mimic the natural singing experience. And acceptance is key; when you're having trouble getting comfortable with head-phones, wedges, or in-ears, the solution isn't to give up, to go crazy, or to be miserable. It is to change your expectations, as well as what you do in response to challenging performance situations.

"The best advice I ever heard regarding any form of vocal performance came from Billie Holiday. When asked how she was able to deliver world-class performances, even with pickup bands that weren't nearly her caliber, Lady Day replied, 'Oh, them? I don't know what they're playing. I'm singing to the music I hear in my head.'"

—Robert Wright, Producer/Engineer, Nashville, Tennessee[7]

Helpful as an attitude adjustment may be, first and foremost you *must* master the tools to the best of your ability, as nothing can compensate for time spent using the technology. Pick up a pair of in-ears (and headphones) as well as an inexpensive microphone and start experimenting at home. The music software GarageBand comes free with all Mac computers and Audacity and Cakewalk can be downloaded inexpensively or for free as well. Head to every possible open mic night and live gig you can book with your in-ears in tow. That way, you won't be trying to learn on the job when your big break comes around.

Even once you've become adept at singing in the live arena, there will inevitably be times when you'll struggle to hear yourself or some aspect of the instrumentation you've come to rely upon. That is why, as Cara mentioned, it's critical to learn how to hear by feeling and sensing your voice.

Sensing Your Voice

"Development of sensory awareness throughout the body as well as the larynx is essential for vocal longevity."

—Joan Lader, Voice Therapist and Vocal Coach[8]

To understand this concept, we first have to remember that using the voice is primarily a reflexive process and that a large part of our work is just getting out of its way. Even advanced training and fine-tuning begin with observation.

When singers instead try to physically and intellectually manhandle their voices, the result is hesitation, overthinking, and strain that you can hear in their instruments, as well as in their language. As I mentioned in *The Art of Singing*, they want to "master the tension" to create agility, understand the "force" that will allow flexibility, and learn to "control" their range of dynamic expression.

Forceful, aggressive approaches are just as unhelpful when it is hard or even impossible to hear yourself. In any environment, working with the voice requires the willingness to surrender the desires for control and perfection, as our only chance of coming close to either is through letting go of both.

Great singers know this. I love sharing the scholarly *Journal of Singing* with students; after article upon article on the technical workings of the voice, it always features an interview with famous singers who nine times out of ten say that they aren't entirely sure how their voices do what they do. And that they surrender even more to the ride when it comes to live performance.

"At some point, you have to stop playing the instrument and start playing music."

—Victor Wooten, Bass Player and Author of *The Music Lesson*[9]

It's not that the physiology of the voice isn't fascinating or academically understandable, or that these singers are clueless. We're talking about some of the top vocalists in the classical field here! Rather, these men and women are acknowledging that some of the most important practical aspects of being a vocalist and a performer are understood on a level that transcends our conscious, logical thinking.

Similarly, our ability to perceive what our voices are doing transcends our hearing. This is news to most of us, who have always relied upon our ears as the sole gauge of our vocal competence and progress. Indeed, few of us have prioritized the wisdom of our sensory system when it comes to singing, though it's often the very thing that will not only get you through a gig, but also will help you to nail it.

> "Right feeling leads to right action. Action follows impulse, with no thought in between."
>
>   —Dr. William Sears[10]

The first step in developing the ability to sense your voice is to simply refocus your attention and energy from hearing to feeling . . . to experience your voice *first* as a sensation. In songs, scales, and even in your speech, start by closely observing how your voice exists in and moves through your body, throat, head, and mouth. Become aware of the sensations of an accurate pitch—the resonance and feel of it when it locks in—as well as when one rubs incorrectly against the music. Get to know the experience of how your support shifts as you move throughout your range. In time, you'll be able to recognize the rightness of your voice production, often before you're actively aware of how you sound.

This doesn't mean that you'll necessarily feel each note clicking into a specific physical spot, though some people have a comparable experience. Instead, you'll have a sure sense of how your voice functions and the well-worn paths it takes to achieve certain outcomes. In time, this active awareness slips into the background, and you're left simply knowing when things are on and when they are off, as well as what needs to shift in order to bring them back into alignment.

As you work on this skill, test your progress by playing your favorite song loudly enough so that you can barely or are unable to hear yourself, and, with a digital recorder or your cell phone, record yourself singing along. Start first in a stationary position—the car and shower are also great places to practice—then try the same exercise while walking or even jogging or dancing (being able to accurately sense your voice and sing while distracted is a great way to know whether you're mastering the skill).

Next, introduce headphones if you have a pair, followed by earbuds or in-ear monitors. Once you've become adept at focusing on the sensations of your voice and relinquishing the "sound first" approach to knowing it fully, you'll be shocked to hear how great you sound, even when you aren't able to hear a thing.

Leaping Before You Look

It's one thing to practice sensing your voice in the privacy of your own home and quite another to contemplate doing so onstage. Even once you've become good at it, the idea of throwing caution to the wind during a live gig can be terrifying.

It takes a tremendous amount of courage to engage your voice fully without necessarily knowing what that engagement will sound like. It's like jumping out of an airplane without first checking your parachute.

Counterintuitive as it may seem, giving your performance 100 percent is the only way you stand a chance of sounding good when you're struggling to hear, just as it is when hearing isn't an issue. If you're well practiced and fully committed, your body and voice will default to the sensations it has learned to trust, whether or not you can hear well.

The alternative isn't a good one. When we allow fear and hesitation to physically manifest, the decrease in energy that so many of us assume will only bring down our volume more often than not brings down our pitch as well.

Learning to Trust

Thankfully, you don't have to jump straight into a live gig. Rehearsals and sound-checks are your opportunity to work out the kinks in your sound and performance, including what to do in the event that you can't hear yourself.

This means—and please pay attention—that you have to give up the desire to look good in your rehearsals and soundchecks! They are not opportunities to show off or gain admiration; they are working sessions designed to help you be at your very best come showtime. Trust me, it is far better to sound ridiculous in front of the ten people on your team and in your band than the hundreds or even thousands of people who will be at your gig.

You therefore have to give every rehearsal and soundcheck your all and to trust your team to tell you plainly how you're doing. No one wants to hear that they're off, but better to hear it in a situation where you can do something about it.

You not only have to trust your team. You also have to trust yourself. Confidence doesn't come from being perfect. Confidence comes from doing your very best and being brave enough to let other people help you to become even better.

Mic Technique

As we've discussed, onstage you rarely have the perspective of what the audience hears. Your mix is the only reference you have and it can be very different from what's going on in the house. This is yet another reason to do your absolute best during soundchecks; they're not just about setting the right levels in your monitor and making sure that you can hear yourself well. They're necessary for the front-of-house team to be able to create the right mix for the audience.

One of the more challenging issues both house and monitor engineers need to address is managing the widest volume, range, and expressive dynamics of your singing. As in the studio, some engineers prefer to deal with these variables on their end, setting compression levels so that you can sing as you normally would at a consistent distance from the microphone.

The majority of live sound engineers, however, want you to help out by modifying your position at least somewhat. Unlike in the studio where you can re-record a section if your vocal gets too hot, overwhelming the signal during a live gig leads to distortion, feedback, and other audio problems that can't always be fixed on the fly. Soundchecks occur in the presence of our self-censors and without the benefit of an audience or the full energy of the band. Bring on the adrenaline, lights, and the action, though, and singers often surprise themselves at how very powerful—and loud—they can become.

You therefore must be able to anticipate in real time how to regulate your signal. Watch a few concert videos and you'll see the majority of vocalists move toward and away from the microphone in an effort to balance the overly loud, soft, and strident aspects of their voices during a performance.

At a more advanced level, mic technique also involves making subtle shifts to your sound (without adversely affecting your vocal technique or health), including nasalizing, darkening, and in other ways manipulating your timbre. These abilities are particularly important when it comes to background vocals, as a good deal of tonal blending is required above and beyond regulating vocal balance and volume.

Television and Touring

So far, we've been talking about live performance as a broad category. Now we're going to look more specifically at television, touring, and spot dates. All are key milestones in achieving and sustaining success as an artist in every genre, each with its own unique rigors that you'll need to consider and manage.

Television

In the live arena, you're always on. Yet when you're doing TV gigs, you're "on" at a much more critical and high-profile level. It's live performance up close and personal, and you have to be prepared.

While vigilance in performance conviction is par for the course for theater and classical singers, commercial artists are often less aware of how important and challenging it can be to remain focused throughout a gig. Pauses between songs, stops to retune, and featured solos all give the illusion that it's okay for artists, background singers, and musicians to take a break from being on as well.

When it comes to TV, or any other video source, this isn't so. Even when you're not the focus of a particular song, there's no telling when the camera is going to head your way and zoom in. When it does, make sure that you're in the zone and really listening to that guitar solo rather than looking at your nails or checking out that good-looking guy in the third row. No matter how unlikely you think it is that the camera will be on you, stay focused from the time you step onstage until the time you step off. If you don't, you'll learn the hard way, by seeing yourself spacing out on a live feed video or recording of your gig.

The same is true for your vocal performance. While a lovely house mix is being created for the studio audience, your microphone is going by direct feed into the television audience's mix, which doesn't have the benefit of the studio ambience, its feel-good vibes, or the same amount of effects, particularly when it's a live broadcast.

Therefore, make sure that you're not only in great vocal shape before a television gig, but also that you're sure your monitoring system will support you. We've all watched certain artists on TV and wondered how it's possible that they sound *that* much different from their records. Obviously some people aren't as talented as technology makes them seem, but by and large, challenges with live sound are the main culprit in causing good singers to sound anywhere from slightly off to altogether awful when it comes to performing on TV.

I'm therefore a fan of wedges whenever possible, which are great in relatively small television-studio spaces. Of course if you're a master with in-ears and your own sound guy is with you, go for it. Otherwise, using them is a gamble that may not be altogether worth making, particularly given that television soundchecks don't always provide for an ample opportunity to lock in your mix.

Another important consideration is that television gigs often occur at tough times, including very early in the morning and very late at night. And they're frequently in different cities; even if you're based in studio-heavy New York or Los Angeles, you're still only local about half of the time. I remember enduring a week of three red-eye flights between the two coasts with gigs at each stop. Most established tours aren't usually quite as brutal, but are nonetheless intense.

On the other end of the scheduling spectrum, there are often large gaps between television performances. For artists, this shouldn't be particularly troublesome as they are generally coupled with tours in support of new projects, ensuring that you're vocally strong and prepared, as well as comfortable with the material.

For background singers and other musicians for hire, however, its always important to be on your toes. Not only will you often be called upon for spot dates and even tours with little notice, but being in good vocal shape also won't always prepare you for the often challenging and out-of-your-sweet-spot vocal parts you may be asked to sing. Therefore, scope out any types of melody lines, licks, and areas of your voice you tend to avoid and work them on a regular basis. That ascending third right at the edge of your comfort zone? Now's the time to make it as familiar and effortless as your go-to song.

Touring

Artists generally either love or hate going on the road. Some thrive living out of a suitcase, sleeping on a bus, and always waking up in a new place. For others, being away from their homes, families, and routines is a disruption and a sacrifice. Both types of people often find it challenging to breathe fresh life into the same material night after night, particularly theater and classical singers who are unable to improvise.

Love it or leave it, touring requires a kind of discipline most new artists don't anticipate. Eager to get on the road, their energy levels and excitement are often so high that any kind of moderation seems completely ridiculous, until about halfway through the tour when voices, health, and relationships start to fall apart.

Tours are like marathons, not sprints. They're intense and rigorous and you have to pace yourself. And not just vocally; you need to ensure that your body, mind, and spirit can go the distance. This isn't easy when you're bouncing between different venues and hotels on a bus or plane numerous times a week. Even when you're having a great time, travel and change are stressful to the body. You have to take extra care of yourself, making sure to stay warm, healthy, and rested.

A big part of staying healthy is staying hydrated. Room-temperature water on a regular basis is the best preemptive medicine money can buy. It's not just the schedule and the partying. Dry hotels and planes, stuffy buses, the dustiness backstage, and weather changes take their toll. Even if you're a saint with a humidifier strapped to your back, the change from your normal daily and dietary habits are often enough to lower your immunity and bring on a cold.

If you're not already into exercise, now's the time to get interested. It's not only great for health; having a bit of a morning or an evening routine is also a nice way to provide some consistency and grounding in an otherwise random schedule. Most hotels and even some motels have decent gyms these days and even a little time on the treadmill to get your blood flowing is beneficial physically and vocally. If there's no gym, go for a quick jog or a walk every morning, or pack a jump rope and resistance bands. I'm also a big believer in the importance of stretching and, thankfully, a fold-up yoga pad takes up very little space in your suitcase.

You also want to make sure to get some quiet, alone time. It can be tempting to sightsee, party, and hang out nonstop with new friends in new places. But just like at home, you need some time to yourself. Make sure you get it. You're not just playing shows with these people . . . you're *living together*. You don't get to go home, be in a bad mood, and get your game face back on before you head to the next gig. First thing in the morning over coffee in the hotel lobby and last thing at night in the elevators or at the hotel bar, you are in it and with one another.

> "Listen to the stage manager and get onstage when they tell you to. No one has time for the rock star act. None of the techs backstage care if you're David Bowie or the milkman. When you act like a jerk, they are completely unimpressed with the infantile display that you might think comes with your dubious status. They were there hours before you building the stage, and they will be there hours after you leave tearing it down. They should get your salary, and you should get theirs."
> —Henry Rollins, Musician, Writer, and Spoken Word Performer[11]

On established tours, including musical theater tours, you're also traveling with the technical crew, who almost always outnumber the artists. For many singers, this is the first time they've interacted so closely with techies and roadies, or at least for an extended period of time. If this is you, take Rollins's words to heart, as they reflect a common and sometimes deserved sentiment among the support team.

While it's not your job to change how every techie and roadie anticipates and relates to the artists with whom they tour, you do want to check yourself and be respectful. Don't be a diva, and make sure to listen *and* think before you speak. I'm not saying to be someone you're not; some people, artists and crew alike, are going to form negative opinions about you regardless of what you do. Gossip is part of the tour life so you might as well get used to it.

Remember that two very different types of people are traveling together on the road, which tends to be fertile ground for the perpetuation of stereotypes we spent a whole section of this book trying to break down. Do your part to help this process by resisting the urge to generalize, as well as to overestimate your own importance and to underestimate theirs. Regardless of whether you think someone's specific job seems important or interesting, every artist and crew member is essential to the show getting up and running. Therefore, treat everyone with the same kindness and respect with which you yourself would like to be treated.

Finally, remember that no tour is in a vacuum, and that you'll likely run into many of the same musicians and techies down the road. It's a small industry and the touring aspect of it is even smaller. Rumors abound and word gets around. So do pictures and videos. Therefore, behave yourself!

A Final Word About Performing and Performance Anxiety

We already addressed performance anxiety in Chapter Five, but we can't talk about live performance without mentioning it again. Artists at every level of the game experience it, and so will you. The physical fight-or-flight mechanism has been in place forever and isn't going anywhere. And the mind puts up a darn good fight as well.

We've talked about where performance anxiety comes from and why it hangs on so tenaciously. We've discussed some tools for handling it, though again, there is no trick to or secret for overcoming performance anxiety. If there were, we'd all read that book and be done with it!

There is *only* one way to get comfortable singing in front of other people, and that is . . . to sing in front of other people. The Police, the Beatles, and Dave Matthews Band all come to mind, acts that spent virtually every night for years gigging live before they even thought about record labels, number-one records, or the Grammys. That's the reason they're such fantastic performers and so comfortable onstage . . . because they were performing *all of the time.*

It's not rocket science. The only way to go from good to great to legendary—as well as from terrified to comfortable—is to get your butt up onstage and pay your dues. You'll still get nervous from time to time, especially when a new milestone or type of gig comes around. But over time, even the momentous events will cease to bring on the sting of panic you may have experienced at the beginning of your career.

Bottom line: if you're calling yourself a singer or an artist, stop avoiding the stage. If you're going to be successful, you'll eventually be on it all of the time. And in the interim, there is simply no other way to hone your chops and to become the best and most comfortable performer you can be . . . and to keep your sanity while doing so.

CHAPTER FOURTEEN

The "Other" Tools

Hopefully, it's now clear how much more is involved in becoming a professional singer than just having a good voice. Mastering your mindset, regularly performing, understanding the technology onstage and in the studio, and being great with the people who run it are all critical.

The Business of Music

There's also the business aspect of the music business to understand, which far too many singers are unfamiliar with. Even some who've been in the game for a long time are often uncertain of its rules, finding themselves frantic whenever opportunities or problems come along.

Part of this is due to an aversion many creative types have to business; an aversion that stems from the common but untrue notion that people are either creative or business-minded, and that the development of one will somehow detract from the other. We talked about this a great deal in The *Art of Singing*, so if you find yourself stuck in this way of thinking, please revisit or take a look at Chapter Five of that book.

Even those who are interested in learning about the business side of things often come up against a lack of practical information. Thankfully, more and more music programs are offering music business classes, yet they still don't always help you know what actual steps to take or how to meet the right people.

I remember asking one of my college music professors about how to start my career, to which she replied, "Just sing and it'll happen!" This is not a strategy. The music business is a *business* after all. Just as singers lose opportunities when they lack the knowledge about today's recording and live performance technology, not knowing how to navigate the professional aspects of your career or how to build the necessary relationships is just as likely to stop you in your tracks.

"Hustle beats talent when talent doesn't hustle."

—Ross Simmonds, Entrepreneur[1]

Fortunately, the information is out there if you're willing to look. As I mentioned before, if you're in the commercial field, Don Passman's *All You Need to Know About the Music Business* is a great place to start, as are ASCAP, BMI and AFTRA. *Backstage* magazine and Actors' Equity are fantastic resources for musical theater singers, and classical artists often begin their professional careers in competitions and summer fellowships and programs, all of which you can find information about online.

The rest of the career-launching equation, in every genre, is hard work and dedication, relentless networking, and honing your craft in practice and performance on a constant, tireless basis.

That said, there are some aspects of the music industry that you just can't discover until you've been in it for a while. I'm not talking about ideal percentages in management contracts or advances in publishing deals, which you can learn about in a book or class. I'm talking about the various people, decisions, and crossroads you'll encounter throughout your career that will test you personally as well as professionally; the difficult and sometimes uncomfortable situations that require the self-awareness and self-trust to stay true to your artistic vision, as well as to yourself.

These situations are challenging for many singers, whose passions often lead them without being tempered by reason and self-reflection. The issues we'll be talking about do not benefit from emotions running the show; in fact, they often cloud the issue. This is about the ability to think calmly, rationally, and logically when faced with some of the most important and pivotal moments of your career.

Here are some of those moments, which friends, clients, colleagues, and I have encountered over the years. There are countless other situations and scenarios in which you may find yourself, but hopefully the discussion will help to prepare you for how to maturely and bravely handle whatever may come your way.

The Art of the Contract

Another book I recommend to commercial artists is Moses Avalon's *Confessions of a Record Producer*. Like Passman's book, it's updated regularly and chock-full of vital information to help you get started and make it in the music business.

It's also a fantastic resource for helping you to recognize and avoid some of its more shady characters.

These types exist in every industry, of course, though in the music business we seem to have more than our fair share. Who knows whether these types are drawn specifically to our industry, or to any field where so many people are desperate for help getting to a location for which there is no good map. All I can tell you is that, at some point, you're going to encounter one or more of them.

On the opposite end of the spectrum, there are also tons of fantastic and well-meaning people who have no business being in the music business. They love you, they love what you do, and they'll do *anything* to help you . . . they just don't necessarily know how.

Different as these two types are, they do have something in common. And that is that they both generally will want you to sign a contract with them.

As I've said before, contracts aren't inherently bad. And who knows, your next-door neighbor's dad might make a great manager. But when you sign them at the wrong time, with the wrong people, or for the wrong reasons—or heaven forbid, all three—then they become problematic.

The Right Time to Sign

So what is the right approach to contracts? When is the right time to sign them and whom should you sign them with?

The *wrong* time to sign a contract is if you think that simply by having a manager, agent, publisher, producer, or any other representative, you will somehow be closer to becoming a successful singer. Having a manager if you have nothing to manage or a publisher if you haven't written a song is rather pointless, and the good ones won't sign you up until you've got something for them to work with.

It's also a bad idea to sign with someone, hoping they'll do the work that you can and should be doing for yourself. Rarely do things worth having come easy, and making it as a professional singer falls into this category. Don't think that a great manager or agent will save you from the grunt work, the dues paying, or living out of a van on your first tour. They won't.

When is the right time to sign a contract with a manager, agent, or publisher then? When they are able to do things for you that you're unable do for yourself, including helping you to gain access to people, places, and other contracts that you can't. Believe me, there's nothing worse than being legally stuck with a B- or C-level player when the A-team comes along to admire all of the hard work you eventually realized no one but you was going to do.

Whether or not you've done your part, *many* people will promise that they know every label president, booking agent, casting director, club manager, and songwriter in the world, and that they will get in touch with them on your behalf. But that doesn't mean they do or they will, in spite of the fact that you may want more than anything to believe them.

There's only one way to find out, and that is to do your homework. Check out their credentials, ask around, and spend some time together, including possibly doing some provisional, noncontractual work to see if they might be a good fit for you and your needs at the current place in your career.

Unfortunately, when we're desperate, we're often afraid to say what we want or to ask the tough questions for fear of losing what we hope to be an opportunity. When you've worked hard for a long time to get ahead with little progress, bringing *someone* onto your team feels like you're getting somewhere! But remember, that step forward you think you're taking can end up being a giant leap backward if you're stuck in a bad contract or relationship.

Hiring an Entertainment Attorney

It's therefore important for you to get to know a good entertainment lawyer for when seemingly attractive proposals do come your way. Of course, these guys don't come cheap, but when you're starting out you can usually negotiate a discounted rate or work with a beginning associate in a reputable firm. Find someone you trust and listen to that person. If he or she tells you that it's a bogus contract—or a bogus person—pay attention.

It's also in your best interest to learn the basics of music contracts early on in your career. Thanks to the Internet, standard versions of publishing, management, and production deals are easy to get your hands on. While you'll still want your attorney to look over anything significant you may be considering, with a bit of research you'll be able to do quite a bit of contract vetting on your own.

I'll say it again: when working with an attorney, *listen*. You're paying this person to have your best interests in mind, regardless of anything to the contrary your potential new friend might say. If he throws a fit because you won't sign the contract exactly as he's presented it, let him. Remember: it's not just about the final deal you may come to and the contract you'll potentially sign. Seeing how your partners-to-be handle the negotiating process will often let you know plain as day whether you're dealing with wolves or sheep.

Unless we're talking about someone established who leaves no doubt as to his or her credentials *and* commitment to working with you, there's no reason you can't at least ask for a bit of flexibility while you get to know each other. How about a six-month trying-it-out period with a new manager? Why not see if this agent will let you work nonexclusively for a while so that you don't lose out on other potential opportunities while you're getting to know each other? How about working with a producer on one track for a fee to make certain that you work well together?

Sometimes they'll say yes, sometimes they'll say no. And then it's your call whether or not you think doing business with them is a good idea. For many of you, this will be the toughest part of the process . . . *making a decision*. How do you know which move is the right one?

You don't. But as you're responsible for your career, you're ultimately responsible for all of the decisions that need to be made in it as well. Sometimes you'll make the right ones, other times not. And there are no guarantees; sometimes the least likely person may be the best manager in the world. Other times, that established agent who promised you the moon will do nothing for you. Be willing to learn from *both* types of experiences and don't beat yourself up if you make the wrong move. Nothing's forever, including a bad contract.

When No Means Yes and Yes Means No

Once in a while you not only meet the right person, but also they love you and want to work with you. Oddly enough, though, you haven't heard back from them after reaching out a couple of times. So you try again, and again, get no response.

Or maybe you do hear back—and guess what? They loved the latest round of songs you sent as well as your video, and they want to hear and see more! So you send them additional material . . . after which they say the same thing.

This "interest limbo" can be one of the most frustrating parts of the business. What you're being told sounds so positive, yet nothing's actually happening. What gives?

It's a lot simpler than you might think. And that is: if people want to work with you, they'll give you a contract, sign you, promote you, or do whatever it is that they do for artists. If they don't, they won't.

But you've had three meetings and they keep asking for more music! They've even taken you to dinner and just last month they sent a junior rep to one of your shows!

I know, I know. But go back and reread the paragraph before last. If they want to work with you, they will. If they don't, they won't. With rare exception, it really is that simple.

If you haven't heard of the popular dating book *He's Just Not That Into You* by Greg Behrendt and Liz Tuccillo, now may be a good time to flip through a copy. Or just let the message of the title sink in, as it applies equally to the music business. As in dating, the proof is in the pudding: no matter what people say, the bottom line is that you're going to get asked out or you're not; they're going to want to see you again, or they won't. The tough part isn't interpreting what is and isn't being said. It's admitting it to yourself and accepting it.

I once went round and round with a publisher whom I liked and respected a great deal for a year. Yet it turns out that what I thought was professional interest was really friendship, a flexible schedule, and a rather large expense account for lunch meetings on his part. Not surprisingly, a contract never materialized—an outcome I probably should have seen coming around month four.

There is a difference between optimism and reality. And while optimism is required in the music business and life, so is the ability to see the writing on the wall when it is staring you plainly in the face. Being positive and persistent will always serve you well. But wasting a lot of time hoping and waiting for what was never going to happen is another thing altogether.

Don't just listen to people's words, *hear what they are saying*. And remember, rather than get upset when things don't go your way, use that energy to pursue other relationships. At some point in the not-so-distant past you didn't know about this person you're now convinced is the only one who can help you to advance your career.

> "Friends and good manners will take you where money won't go."
>
> —Margaret Walker

There are exceptions to every rule, and occasionally, people who are genuinely interested in working with you won't get back in touch for a long time. Sometimes people are indeed that busy, or perhaps they are waiting to see what you'll do with the feedback they've given you about your music or career.

The music business is all about relationships. And today, those relationships often begin and gain momentum over the phone and e-mail. Just because you aren't hearing from that agent or manager doesn't mean that they don't read or listen to your messages—or hear about them from their staff. So always be kind and respectful, even when you assume you've been written off or think no one is paying attention.

Saying Yes to (Almost) Everything

"For every yes, something is created. For every no, there is no creation. The person I am right now is the accumulation of my yeses and nos over the course of my life, and that is true for each and every one of us."

—Don Miguel Ruiz Jr., Author, *The Five Levels of Attachment*[2]

So often today I meet singers who, while they're not sure of what the "right" path to making it is, have heard all about or are certain of what the wrong ones are.

The current "wrong step" is to audition for *American Idol, The Voice, America's Got Talent,* or any other television show where—heaven forbid—you could get invaluable experience, gain international attention, and possibly launch your career overnight.

Hopefully my sarcasm is coming through loud and clear. . . .

Are there some legitimate downsides to being on these shows or ones like them? Perhaps, though none that I'm aware of. Even if you're an artist with a very organic, noncommercial type of music that the show won't feature, is it *really* a bad thing to audition? What's the worst thing that can happen? You make it, get on TV singing covers as well as possibly one or more of your own songs, gain a ton of fans, and become well known. You're telling me that won't help you on your own artistic journey?

The same strong opinions exist about whether artists should record jingles, do industrial work, perform on a cruise ship, or sing background vocals for other artists while working toward their solo careers. In fact, the film *20 Feet from Stardom* recently highlighted Judith Hill's debate over whether or not to give up her gigs singing backup for Elton John and others in order to pursue her own project.

In some instances, turning down certain opportunities might enable you to focus on and dedicate time to your own career. That said, there is no "right" path to becoming a successful singer, and you never know what gigs will turn out to be helpful and which ones won't. In my experience, it's often the random, seemingly off-track choices that end up leading artists to the very success they've been searching for all along.

Therefore, my advice is to say yes to everything. If the opportunity is with a reputable company, the contract is sound and fair, and it will expand you as an artist and a person, you'll be in good shape no matter what happens. At the very least, you'll meet new people, have a new experience, and learn something.

Finding Your Trusted Five

"Take criticism seriously, but not personally."

—Hillary Clinton[3]

That doesn't mean that saying yes is always easy. Most singers wrestle with even the simple aspects of their careers, so deciding whether or not they should take a giant leap in a previously unthought-of direction can be nerve-racking. Add into the mix the dizzying array of contradictory opinions from people you do and don't know about your songs, website, marketing, and who knows what else, and it's a wonder that anyone chooses anything!

The best way to filter out the useful from the useless opinions is to carefully select a group of people who will act as your advisers. Take your time finding these people and give each one a good deal of thought. You're looking for expertise and objectivity. You want people willing to tell you the hard truths, and knowledgeable enough to know how to steer you in the right direction when you're heading or thinking of heading off course. Most importantly, you want men and women you know and trust, whose careers you respect as much as you respect who they are as people.

Find these people, listen to them, and for the most part, thank everyone else for their opinion.

In my experience, five is the perfect number. It's a large enough group to allow for a healthy debate when they disagree, and small enough to come to a consensus about what the best course of action might be.

The alternative is to listen to and internalize every opinion that comes your way, which is a big mistake. Not only are critics ruthless (and often off base), but also today everyone has a public viewpoint, which they are more than eager to share on Facebook, in their blogs, and on all your YouTube videos. I'm not saying that you want to hide from what people are saying about you. I'm telling you that the best way to get honest, productive feedback is to find and work with a small, knowledgeable group of people who are as invested in your success as you are.

Three Golden Rules

We all know that to make it in this business, you need to have some amount of talent. But how you behave is just as important. That might sound like nothing more than a nice idea to those of you just starting out, but as you climb the ranks, you'll start to notice that those in charge are not only looking for great musicians and artists, but people they like to be around as well.

While I can't sum up how to be a likeable person in three bullet points, give the following ideas some thought and take as much of it as you can on board. They'll take you far personally and professionally.

Listen Before You Speak

"I make sure that when I speak, I ask myself, 'Is it necessary?' 'Is it true?' 'Is it kind?' 'Will it make a difference?' Otherwise, I don't speak."

—Deepak Chopra[4]

I love the saying that we have two ears and one mouth for a reason . . . so that we might listen twice as much as we speak.

In every conversation and in every relationship, it is always best to start by listening. *Always.* That's the only way you'll get to know people as well as what matters to them. And when you speak to what they care about, the conversation—and the relationship—will almost certainly get off to a good start.

This is particularly the case when you're in a new musical environment. Every studio, every technical team, and every company has a way of doing business and interacting. They have their own interpersonal dynamics and sense of etiquette. Listening is *the* tool that allows you to learn their ways before you open your mouth to share yours.

You may have a certain process and a fantastic creative vision. And there will be time enough to share them . . . when the time is right. When you walk into a room assuming there is more for you to learn than there is for you to offer or teach—no matter how certain you may be about things—you'll be amazed at how quickly people become interested in what you have to say.

Burn No Bridges

> "Be nice to people on your way up because you'll meet them on your way down."
> —Wilson Mizner, Playwright and Entrepreneur[5]

Success isn't a one-way street. In every business, success *and* failure are a part of the journey and anyone who's ever spent any time in the music business knows this to be true. No matter how high up on the food chain you may be, you're always only one hit record, production, tour, or TV gig away from being unemployed.

Still, people climbing the ladder of success often leave one rung assuming that they'll never see it again. Or anyone else at that level. And they often treat them accordingly.

Big mistake.

> "Great minds discuss ideas, average minds discuss events, small minds discuss people."
> —Eleanor Roosevelt

The vast majority of truly successful people I've worked with are incredibly kind and generous. Not because they had to be to get ahead, but because they are genuinely that way. Their talent has taken them far, and their kindness and goodness even further.

Follow their example. Treat every person at every point along your journey with kindness and respect. Not just because you *should*, but also because you can. This includes how you speak about them when they're not there. It's so easy to confuse gossip with conversation, but they're not the same thing. Say only the types of things about others that you'd like said about you. And as the saying goes, if you have nothing good to say, keep your mouth shut.

If you're prone to gossip or can't seem to shake the habit, take a good look in the mirror; usually the only reason we look down on other people and talk negatively about them is if we're struggling with adequacy issues of our own.

Lighten Up

"The more we project emotional or psychological limitations onto the voice, the harder it is to play. Indeed, the voice prefers to be held as a selfless instrument. And when we imagine the voice (as such) instead of a mythical Holy Grail for which we must constantly search, it becomes something we can actually approach, work with, and refine."

—Silvia Nakkach, Author, *Free Your Voice*[6]

There is a big difference between being serious about what you do and taking yourself too seriously. Far too many people confuse the two. Earlier we talked about the difference between commitment and attachment. I'll say it again: Commitment will take you far and allow you to enjoy the journey. Attachment will have you running in circles and give you a headache.

You can always tell which path you're on by the flavor of your feelings. If you're fearful, controlling, panicked, jealous, competitive, or small in any way, it's time to reassess your approach and make a change. None of these feelings or the behaviors they inspire is going to help you to advance your career (at least, not in the long run).

I recently went to see a client in a leading role on Broadway that she'd been understudying for years. She was *fantastic*. Yet in speaking with her backstage, she simply couldn't see that. All she was thinking about was one note—one note in the course of an entire show—that she felt didn't have enough energy. It wasn't off. It wasn't ugly. But in her mind, and in her mind alone, it was just a little too quiet. She was so obsessed with this one note that she missed the fans outside asking for her autograph and the congratulations of her castmates as she made her way into a cab.

This type of behavior is so common in our field that it's seen as normal. But it shouldn't be. Creativity doesn't require you to be a wreck. If you find yourself freaking out at the idea of an off note, panicking when someone doesn't return your call, or losing it just before an audition, stop, breathe, and lighten up.

The Casting Couch

"If you want to sleep your way to the top, fine. But if you want to make it without doing that, there's still a very fine line you have to play. You can't be all business. You can't be a wet blanket on their party. You've gotta look good. You can't turn them off. Otherwise, they'll get someone else. You don't have to have sex with people. But you do have to have the promise of it out there sometimes."

—Michelle, Recording Artist, Los Angeles, California[7]

At the beginning of my career, I was fortunate to be introduced to a rather well-known artist. After a few years of working hard in home and smaller studios, I found myself in the heart of New York City's music scene, spending evenings in a top studio singing and playing piano with famous musicians and singers on real records.

Terrific as the experience was, I also got my first glimpses into some less than ideal sides of the music business, including excessive drinking and drugs, unbelievable displays of dishonesty and disloyalty, and the prevalence of the "casting couch."

Here are a few things that happened to me in that one experience alone:

- Instead of taking the subway after a late-night session, the artist insisted that his driver take me home. Ten minutes into the drive, the artist called, apparently expecting phone sex in exchange for the ride.
- I was in the studio bathroom one afternoon when the locked door flew open and he tried to make out with me. There I was, twenty-one years old and washing my hands, only to find a grown, married man walking through the door with his lips puckered up.
- Finally, I was told—in almost as many words—that if I wanted to showcase for the president of his record label, sex would be expected in return.

I remember that showcase like it was yesterday. I sat in the audience watching the girls who did choose to make that exchange with a great deal of sadness, for them as well as for myself. After the final singer's set, I walked out and never went back.

> "Sometimes I wonder . . . why bother working your ass off to get to the middle when it seems so much easier to screw your way to the top?"
> —Erica H., Singer, Songwriter, and Actress[8]

Why didn't I leave earlier? Why didn't I go right away, after the artist's first advance? Because I was shocked and in denial. And because I was young, hungry, and desperate to pursue my dream. I wasn't about to respond to his sexual advances to further my career. Yet I also didn't want to give up on what seemed like a great opportunity when I could simply hang up the phone or walk out of the bathroom. Especially when, as I later learned, the same type of thing happens in cars, bathrooms, and recording studios around the world.

And that's why I'm sharing this story. My first major professional experience wasn't an anomaly. I could dedicate an entire chapter to the come-ons and downright ultimatums that I and others have encountered at every stage of our careers in exchange for record deals, live gigs, and other professional advancements. Some say yes and get ahead (or don't—none of the girls who showcased that day in New York got deals). Others say no, and many well-earned and well-deserved breaks and opportunities are missed because of it.

> "It's not right, but it's okay. I'm gonna make it anyway."
> —Whitney Houston from *My Love Is Your Love*[9]

The casting couch is a very real aspect of not only the music business, but of many businesses where such a large number of people are vying for so few spots. It's supply and demand; those holding the keys to any coveted kingdom start to realize that some are willing to do whatever it takes to get in. And they exploit that. In the words of one such record label vice president after I sang for him in his office—and I am not making this up: "You're cute and you're talented. Just like a thousand other girls. So give me a blow job and I'll think about it."

Of course, there are plenty of wonderful executives, managers, producers, and others in power who would never dream of behaving this way. Still, you'll likely come across a few predators in your career. When you do, don't give up or let them get you down; instead, focus on using your talents and strengths to create what matters to you. At the end of the day, and at the end of your life looking back, you won't regret the extra work, time, and effort it takes to follow your dreams with integrity.

Getting Screwed with Your Clothes On

Sex isn't the only way you can get screwed in the music business. As I said a moment ago, anytime a large number of people are vying for a small number of spots, things can get a bit shady. This is true whenever money, power, or fame are on the line; those with the ability to grant them seem to hold all the cards and can therefore ask for the moon.

And as we're dealing with all three in the music business, the asking often gets a bit out of hand.

This is often the case when it comes to songwriting and publishing. There are countless artists who will only use a writer's song in exchange for publishing and even songwriting credit. Or slightly more subtly, writers who will only be granted a sliver of the songwriting pie even when they've done the majority or even all of the work.

In my early writing days, I remember getting 20 percent of the credit for a song I wrote half of. The other 80 percent was split by the artist I wrote the song with and his cousin . . . who was in China at the time!

Livid, I consulted a lawyer to figure out how to be properly compensated. Instead, I got a lesson in the cold hard facts: if I wanted the song on the record, I had to accept the 20 percent deal. Otherwise, I'd end up with 50 percent of nothing.

Fair or not, it's what's called paying your dues. Whether it's the song you wrote that you're not getting credit for, the publishing you had to give up in exchange for getting your song to the artist, or the agent or manager who will get you into the audition only if you sign a year-long exclusive contract, in order to get ahead you often have to give up something.

I can't tell you whether you should accept these kinds of offers—that's up to you. But before making your choice, you may want to come to terms with what is a relatively standard though not necessarily ethical practice in the music business, and weigh that against what opportunities might—and might not—come if you do or don't accept it.

Giving up 50 percent of your song might not be a bad deal if a lucrative publishing or artist contract comes from it. Not getting paid union wages to sing backup on a record might mean nothing when it comes to the exposure and money you'd receive from going on the world tour. Doing that voice-over for a buyout rate may be the very thing you need on your reel and résumé to land an even bigger and better-paying job.

Again, there is no right answer. You have every right to refuse to play by anything but the fairest of rules. That said, you may want to consider giving up a bit in the short term to reach your goals down the road. How much and to what degree is up to you.

When to Say No

Early in my career, I worked with a very well-known Broadway agent. I was incredibly lucky to be introduced to him by a fellow singer, and luckier still that he was willing to take me on. Soon after, I was auditioning privately for some of the biggest casting agents and shows on Broadway, and getting lots of great feedback and attention.

Around the same time that he and I began working together, an opportunity came up in Nashville that I didn't want to pass up. And while I could understand that he might be against the plan given our focus on theater, I was shocked when he started screaming and insulting me when I gave him the news.

When people cross the line, I have no problem telling them to take a hike, which is exactly what I did with this still very well-known agent. It's just not in my nature to allow someone to insult and be nasty to me.

I'm well aware that this isn't the case for everyone, though. We all have our issues, and some people succumb and are even drawn to this type of treatment.

Abuse of any kind is a very real and very terrible problem. And while some relationships begin with blatant mistreatment, in others it often starts so subtly that we don't realize there is an issue until we are weakened body and soul. At which point, it can not only be hard to leave the situation, but also to undo the world of hurt that many come to believe they deserve.

We teach young children to just say no . . . to drugs, to being touched inappropriately, to strangers offering candy and rides. I'm giving you the same advice. When someone threatens or disrespects you, when you see that glimmer of rage in someone's eye that transcends a bad mood or a bad day, walk away. Even if it takes every fiber of your being, do not allow yourself to work, spend time with, or become intimate with people who leave you feeling worse about yourself when you are with them.

No amount of success, attention, or money is worth trading your heart and soul for.

Embracing Plan B

"Great ideas are captivating, but great businesses are self-sustaining."
—Robert Safian, Editor, *Fast Company* magazine[10]

At the beginning of the chapter I mentioned that singers are often wary of developing their business sense for fear of detracting from their creativity, and nowhere is this mindset more prevalent than when it comes to what singers do to pay the bills. To many, the idea of having a "real job" while working on their music seems ridiculous; how could they possibly give 100 percent to both? Better to do something unimportant so that they can put all of their energy into singing.

But think about it. If you're working twenty, thirty, or forty hours a week to pay the bills, you're giving your all to your day job, even if your mind and heart aren't totally there. And in fact, being somewhere you don't want to be drains more energy than doing something you enjoy.

So why not do something that inspires you, as well as builds your economic situation?

The answer, once again: scarcity-based thinking.

For many people, the thought of having a lucrative career in addition to pursuing their music seems impossible. After all, working on Plan B is widely known to be the worst thing you can do if you want to achieve Plan A.

Popular as this sentiment may be, it's not true. Are you telling me that you can't be a successful singer *and* own real estate? You're saying you can't be a fantastic songwriter if you've started a side business? Or that you can't pursue an online education or do some freelance Internet-based work while on a Broadway tour?

Of course you can! And not only will you be inspired and challenged in new ways, but you'll also generate more money than you would at any old nine-to-five, freeing up even more time and energy to focus on your music.

Perhaps most importantly, you'll deal with any fears, insecurities, and doubts you may have about your ability to build and run a business. There is a big difference between what we *can't do* and what we *don't yet know how to do*, and most of us confuse the two. Given that your music career is in fact a business, you might as well embrace every opportunity to learn the skills and test them out in the real world as soon as possible.

Before you protest that no one does this, or that you're too busy to even consider taking on something "so big" as another career, add up all the time you spend on Facebook, watching TV, and otherwise goofing off—as well as stressing out and complaining about your financial situation—and imagine the countless income-generating ideas you could be working on and implementing instead. This includes ventures involving music, for those of you who insist that you're not good at or interested in anything else.

If you're not willing to give this a try, do yourself a favor and at least get a day job in your own field. Why waitress or work at a clothing store when plenty of record labels, music magazines, theaters, and recording studios need secretaries, assistants, staff, and interns? If you're going to spend forty hours a week doing *something* to pay the bills, at least be in an environment where you're likely to meet and be around people who can actually help you with your music.

PART FOUR

Beginning the Show

CHAPTER FIFTEEN

A Brave New World

"Twenty years from now you will be more disappointed by the things that you didn't do than by the ones you did do. So throw off the bowlines. Sail away from the safe harbor. Catch the trade winds in your sails. Explore. Dream. Discover."
—H. Jackson Brown Jr., Author[1]

Thinking about this chapter, I initially pictured a pretty traditional recap of all that we've been discussing.

But really, everything has already been covered.

So instead, this is a note of well wishing. And a reminder of what's important.

Passion

"We're not supposed to do it perfectly. We're just supposed to do it with heart."
—Allison Moorer, Singer/Songwriter[2]

First, I want you to remember why you do what you do . . . and to forget everything else.

If you struggle with a fear of performing; if you drive yourself nuts with perfectionism and feelings of inadequacy . . . If you've lost the joy of singing because you've attached your ego and pride to the process; if your identity and self-worth seem like buoys bobbing on the water with every rise and fall of your career . . .

Remember that at some point you were in love with music. Once upon a time, you were passionate about singing for no other reason than it made you feel good and warmed your heart. It made you happy.

It doesn't matter how long you've been lost. You can return there at any moment. And when you do, make the decision to no longer tolerate departures from that precious place, whether occasional or constant.

You have a say in your relationship with your voice. And it is a *relationship*. It's not some pawn to be toyed with and disregarded. It is a patient and constant gift that deserves the best you have to offer. Therefore, demand more of yourself in the relationship; treat your voice as you would your closest friend or dearest love. Honor and respect your expression. By doing so, you honor and respect yourself.

That's not to say the relationship will always be easy, particularly when you've decided to make a living with your voice. Yet pursuing a career in music—or any career—is a choice, one that you can "unmake" any time. Choose it, or choose something else. Don't linger in the in-between. That valley is a breeding ground for inaction and stagnation, as well as for regret.

Remember to let go of your expectations. We all have an idea of how our careers *should* go and how people *should* act. But things don't always work out according to our wishes and desires. I'm not telling you to be apathetic, to let people walk all over you, or to give up on your greatest goals. What I am telling you is that by letting go of the control and the anxiety that so often come with expectations, you'll be able to more effectively channel your energy into productive action.

Whatever you hope to achieve, make your plans wisely and follow them to the best of your ability. You've only got one shot at this thing called life, so go for it. Only you know how hard you're willing to fight for what you say matters to you. Do that, and then some.

And please, don't let your disappointments, whether big or small, be the reason or the excuse for why you give up on your dreams. If the day comes when you're ready to move on and do something else, as I said, go ahead, without resentment or regret. If not—if you're in it for the long haul—learn how to deal with frustration, keep your chin up, and keep pushing. Whatever path you take in life, think about how you'd like to feel at the end of it looking back, and act from that perspective.

Relationships

Remember that in any career, and in all areas of life, relationships are *everything*. We live in an interconnected world; we are social creatures. How you choose to treat people will always have a direct impact on any and every measure of success you hold to be important.

Therefore, invest in people. Not as a means to an end, but as its own very important goal. In Nashville early in my career, I was initially shocked by how much time people wanted to chat about this and that before getting down to business. Days, weeks, and sometimes *months!*

Now I understand what was really going on. They weren't wasting time; they were building the foundation of trust and friendship upon which everything else would eventually rest.

You can create this foundation with anyone. No matter how different other people may be, no matter how much you may seem to disagree, we are all hungry for meaningful connection. And we have so much more in common than we realize. Look for those commonalities, open your heart, and share yourself.

Lifelong Learning

"Without humility, you are unable to learn."
   —Laszlo Bock, Senior Vice President of People Operations, Google[3]

Finally, I want to leave you with one of the most important lessons I've learned in my life. It's a cornerstone of my approach to singing and teaching, as well as living. And that is to embrace being a perpetual student.

"Maybe you are successful already. Congratulations. Then you know as well as I do that the lessons never stop. We are all students of life until the lights go out on us."

—Farrah Gray, Author and Investor[4]

When legendary cellist Pablo Casals was asked why he continued to practice at age ninety, he replied, "Because I think I'm making progress."

As a culture, we revere experts and masters. Yet those who are at the top of their games are some of the most easygoing, humble, and (wonderfully) childlike people around. Richard Branson, Victor Wooten, and Warren Buffett come to mind, but pick anyone who has truly made it, and you'll often see a sparkle in their eye and a smile on their face that come from being more interested in learning and having fun than knowing everything and being right.

Success—true success—is a by-product of wonder, which rushes in when you embrace the liberating experiences of *not knowing* and *not being perfect*. When curiosity is your guide, there is no negative twinge to failure; there is no fear in the face of the new and the unknown. When you set aside your pride and ego and let your passion lead the way, life becomes a truly thrilling and fulfilling adventure.

Enjoy your life. Enjoy the adventure. And please let me know how it goes!

Notes

Introduction

[1] Carrie Manolakos interview, Fall Voice Conference, NYU School of Medicine, October 4–6, 2012.

[2] Silvia Nakkach, *Free Your Voice: Awaken to Life Through Singing* (Louisville, CO: Sounds True, 2012), 52.

[3] Personal conversation, April 2013.

[4] While classical and musical theater singers today may not interact with technology in performance as directly or often as those in the commercial realm, they certainly do in recording.

[5] David Mellor, *How To Become a Recording Engineer, Part 1: Tips & Techniques, Sound on Sound* magazine, April 1999.

[6] Risa Binder, *Nashville*, Warehouse Records, released August 1, 2014.

[7] Forgive the occasional redundancy in the book; I address some issues more than once, in the hopes that those who only read a section or two will still benefit from the information.

[8] Henri Poincaré, *The Value of Science: Essential Writings of Henri Poincaré*, (New York, NY: Modern Library, 2001).

[9] Alexandre Dumas, French dramatist and novelist, 1802–1870.

[10] Lee Flier, Music Player Network: *Opinions on Female Sound Engineers?* Posted September 13, 2000.

[11] E-mail correspondence, July 6, 2012.

[12] If you were irked by this paragraph, please remember what I said about generalizations! I'm using them as a means to the end of learning, not as a hard and fast rule of how all people are.

Chapter One

[1] Diane Ackerman interview on Public Radio International's program *Innovation Hub*, "A Human Epoch," March 19, 2015.

[2] Diane Ackerman interview on Public Radio International's program *Innovation Hub*, "A Human Epoch," March 19, 2015.

[3] Thomas Mann, *The Magic Mountain* (New York, NY: Alfred A. Knopf, 1927).

[4] To be historically accurate, the actual number of football fields would be much greater. I've arbitrarily chosen one hundred to simplify the metaphor.

[5] This is true even for those born into a digital world.

[6] Albert Einstein, Address to a Students' Disarmament Meeting, 1930.

Chapter Two

[1] While writing and, to a lesser degree, art have come to share the spotlight with speech, for centuries the voice was the primary vehicle for communication.

[2] Along with the collective or group voice, drums have also been used throughout time to agitate and create fear in foes, while exciting and enlivening in-group members. Both vocal and drumming percussion—along with the natural amplification of large numbers of people—created a literal army of sound that increased a group's energy, vibration, and power.

[3] Public domain based on a poem "The Star" by Jane Taylor (from her book *Rhymes for the Nursery* published in 1806).

[4] "Imagine," Copyright John Lennon, 1971.

[5] E-mail correspondence, November 11, 2013.

[6] Interestingly, it doesn't matter whether the sensory trigger or emotional reaction comes first. Whether music is attached to an emotional experience (as in a wedding) or an emotional experience is attached to music (a moving concert), the two become intertwined and form an imprint in our memories. Even in the absence of an emotional experience, music has the ability to produce a memory imprint.

[7] Band-Aid Brand adhesive bandages, Johnson & Johnson.

[8] Oscar Mayer hot dogs.

[9] Mattress Discounters mattresses.

[10] Ted Kerasote, *Merle's Door: Lessons from a Freethinking Dog* (New York, NY: Mariner Books, 2008), 281.

[11] This is true save for certain monkeys, which have demonstrated similar cognitive abilities.

Chapter Three

[1] Or in the instance of warning and warring, to declare their separation.

[2] Stephen R. Covey, *The 7 Habits of Highly Effective People: Powerful Lessons in Personal Change* (London: Simon Schuster Ltd. UK, 1990), 251.

[3] Our Western handshake and eye contact is a similar, though more physically removed, legacy.

[4] Shifts in communication occurred at different times in various parts of the world. Tribal cultures, for example, retained the ancestral type of communication far longer than developing, urban societies. Thus, the contrast between the Native Americans and the Europeans who initially came to their shores. Many mystical traditions today still are wary of technology, including the use of photography.

Chapter Four

[1] Silvia Nakkach, *Free Your Voice: Awaken to Life Through Singing* (Louisville, CO: Sounds True, 2012), 56–57.

[2] Adapted from Alva Noë, *Out of Our Heads: Why You Are Not Your Brain, and Other Lessons from the Biology of Consciousness* (New York, NY: Hill and Wang, 2010), 48.

[3] If you are interested, *The Art of Singing* details a body-led approach to singing.

[4] Dictionary.com.

[5] E-mail correspondence, August 8, 2015.

[6] *The Art of Singing* includes a chapter on language and its difficulty in fully encompassing much of what we wish to express.

[7] Twitter, @DeepakChopra, 9/22/15.

[8] In addition to cortisol and adrenaline, we also get a kick of dopamine once we've achieved our goal.

[9] Silvia Nakkach, *Free Your Voice: Awaken to Life Through Singing* (Louisville, CO: Sounds True, 2012), 57–58.

[10] A hot topic in psychology recently has been the fixed versus growth mindset, and how the latter ensures a healthy relationship with both learning and self-esteem. For an excellent overview of the subject by CDBaby founder Derek Sivers, visit http://sivers.org/failure.

[11] Osho, *My Way: The Way of the White Clouds* (Osho International Foundation: Switzerland, 1974).

Chapter Five

[1] E-mail correspondence, April 2, 2013.

[2] E-mail correspondence, March 1, 2014.

[3] The melody and chord structure of the song were complete; I was looking for someone to produce or arrange and put instrumentation to it.

[4] All names have been changed, save for those who are directly quoted.

[5] For a more complete understanding of songwriting, publishing, production, and licensing—as well as management and record label deals—there are a number of great books and resources out there. One of my favorites is *All You Need to Know About the Music Business* by Donald S. Passman. A new edition is released virtually every year to keep up with the current issues and challenges in the ever-evolving music industry.

[6] Pro Tools is a leading audio recording, mixing, and editing software package developed and manufactured by Avid Technology. We'll be discussing software, mixing, and all of the other audio terms and tools from this chapter in detail in the next section.

[7] A song plugger, like a publishing company, acts on behalf of songwriters, placing songs with recording artists, in film, on television, and in other income-generating mediums.

[8] E-mail correspondence, October 20, 2011.

[9] While you may want to bring people to your sessions, many producers and engineers have their own process when it comes to recording. It's therefore always a good idea to ask whether it is okay to bring coaches, friends, or anyone else to the studio before inviting them.

[10] Shadow or ghost tracks are vocal takes that, when blended with a lead singer's vocal, augment and improve the overall sound. Enough of the lead vocalist's voice remains in the track so that the listener "hears" the voice of the artist, though in fact, the majority of the vocal heavy lifting is being done by the shadow singer. And as with ghostwriters of books, the practice is more widespread than the majority of listeners, and readers, are aware.

[11] The ability to "hear by feel" allows a singer to vocalize consistently, comfortably, and healthily in any sonic environment. It also allows for the development of a more intuitive vocal relationship, which decreases the tension that comes from trying to physically "find" notes. We'll be discussing this skill further in the next section.

Chapter Six

[1] E-mail correspondence, June 27, 2013.

[2] E-mail correspondence, June 27, 2013.

[3] Personal conversation, May 13, 2013.

[4] While the terms *right-brain* and *left-brain* are commonly used to describe creative and technical thinking, respectively, they are not actually lobe specific. Many different areas of the brain work together to facilitate the majority of our thoughts and emotions. And again: remember that these are generalizations! One or two engineers I've worked with are true "right brainers," and I've known a few singers who are as intellectual and technical as they come when it's time to perform. The key is to learn to recognize and work around differences in communication styles.

5 E-mail correspondence, November 15, 2009.

6 Tyley Ross interview, Fall Voice Conference, NYU School of Medicine, October 4–6, 2012.

7 Interestingly, the vocal folds also come together in some instances when we are not using our voices, including times when we are reading, thinking, and even dreaming. Called *subvocalization*, this phenomenon occurs because our linguistic abilities are tied—even in silence—to the physiology of phonation.

8 E-mail correspondence, April 10, 2014.

9 The vocal folds vibrate faster and slower for higher and lower notes, respectively. They do not move up and down on a vertical plane. Still, our minds tend to hold to this up and down association, given that we depict notes as "high" and "low" in our language as well as in musical notation.

10 Nikki James interview, Fall Voice Conference, NYU School of Medicine, October 4–6, 2012.

11 *Bleed* is the term used to describe sound escaping from the headphones into the microphone, which interferes with capturing a clean performance.

12 Joan Lader interview, Fall Voice Conference, NYU School of Medicine, October 4–6, 2012.

13 Another production-related issue involves slowing down or speeding up a song, which—particularly with tape—can lower or raise the song's pitch. Many instrumentalists are able to tune to a variety of microtones and play as they would in a standard key. Singers, however, often can't find these "in between" notes, especially those with perfect or great relative pitch, and can spend an entire session warbling between the two closest tones.

14 E-mail correspondence, December 18, 2013.

15 Maureen Dowd, *New York Times*, "Here's Comes Nobody," May 19, 2012.

16 Brian Regnier, Landmark Insights, *The Power of Listening*. Captured November 13, 2014: http://landmarkinsights.com/2014/09/the-power-of-listening/.

17 *The Philadelphia Story*, written by Donald Ogden Stewart and Philip Barry. Released in 1940, MGM Studios.

Chapter Seven

1 Personal conversation, May 13, 2013.

2 *The Leonard Lopate Show*, WNYC, September 10, 2014.

3 Hambleton, Laura, *The Washington Post*, "A Man with a funny name hasn't stopped singing," December 15, 2015.

4 In a *speculation deal*—whether with a record label, producer, or studio—the artist is given the opportunity to record a number of songs for little or no up-front cost in exchange for the label, producer, or studio's involvement in any deals and income that might be generated from the project.

5 Jessica Strawser, *Writer's Digest*, "Before and After," September 2015, p. 5.

6 Personal conversation, April 2013.

7 E-mail correspondence, December 18, 2013.

8 Tony Robbins via Twitter, @TonyRobbins, April 17, 2012.

9 Vishen Lakhiani, "World's Greatest Workplace," TEDx Ajman, August 8, 2012.

10 Viktor E. Frankl, *Man's Search for Meaning* (New York, NY: Touchstone, 1984), 116.

Chapter Eight

1 Adapted from Daniel Gilbert, "He Who Cast the First Stone Probably Didn't," *New York Times*, July 24, 2006.

2 Yann Martel on *The Diane Rehm Show,* NPR, February 8, 2016.

3 Harper Lee, *To Kill a Mockingbird* (New York, NY: Grand Central Publishing, 1988), 232.

4 Viktor E. Frankl, *Man's Search for Meaning* (New York, NY: Touchstone, 1984).

5 Don Miguel Ruiz, *The Four Agreements: A Practical Guide to Personal Freedom* (San Rafael, California: Amber-Allen Publishing, 1997), 103.

6 C R Strahan, *The Roan Maverick* (Charleston, South Carolina: BookSurge Publishing, 2006), 162.

7 Mahatma Gandhi, *All Men Are Brothers: Autobiographical Reflections* (Navjivan, India: Navjivan Trust, 1995).

8 Including: *The Free Dictionary.* Retrieved March 28, 2013. www.thefreedictionary.com and *Merriam-Webster,* an Encyclopedia Britannica Company. Retrieved March 28, 2013. www.merriam-webster.com

9 E-mail correspondence, October 10, 2013.

10 If you're unfamiliar with EQ, or any of the other terms in this section, feel free to jump ahead to Chapter Twelve for explanations.

11 The speakers are positioned and wired so that the sound of one speaker cancels out the sound from the other as their sounds reach the microphone.

12 E-mail correspondence, October 20, 2011.

13 These agreements also prevent undesired recordings from popping up commercially, as well as terrific ones from being exploited without consent.

14 Georgia Middleman, "Blue Sky Riders: A Total Departure from My Early Years in Nashville," *The Huffington Post,* May 5, 2012.

15 Sara Bareilles, "Brave," *The Blessed Unrest,* © Epic Records, July 12, 2013.

Chapter Nine

1 Ram Dass, *Be Here Now* (New York, NY: Lama Foundation, 1971).

2 J. K. Rowling, *Harry Potter and the Chamber of Secrets* (New York, NY: Scholastic, 2000), 333,

3 On a more extreme note, many children I've worked with in the foster case system who are shuffled from one unhealthy and even abusive foster family to another not only do not trust, they are and know themselves to be untrusting, jaded, and wary . . . even decades after they've left the system.

4 Again, as we discussed in Chapter Seven, the terms "right brain" and "left brain" are more helpful descriptions than wholly accurate locations of where creative and technical brain activity are generated.

5 Susan Trott, *The Holy Man* (New York, NY: Riverhead Books, 1996), 90.

Chapter Ten

1 This scarcity-based model of thinking is discussed in "The Brain in Music" chapter in *The Art of Singing.* In essence, people believe that they are either creative or technical, and that to develop their weaker attribute will somehow detract from the stronger one. This isn't the case.

2 Commercial music is a category that includes R&B, country, rock, rap, and pop music.

3 Publishing companies focus on securing placement of their clients' music in film, television, and other media as well as with recording artists. Administrators, either separate entities or an aspect of a publishing house, work on behalf of songwriters and composers to collect fees for the use of their works.

⁴ The Top 10 artists in descending order were: Bob Dylan, John Lennon/Paul McCartney, John Lennon, Bruce Springsteen, Paul McCartney, Neil Young, Mick Jagger/Keith Richards, Paul Simon, Joni Mitchell, and Elton John/Bernie Taupin.

⁵ Timbaland, Dr. Luke, Pharrell, Max Martin, Rob Thomas, Alicia Keys, Akon, Scott Storch, Stargate, R. Kelly, will.i.am, Ludacris, Kanye West, Chad Kroeger, Taylor Swift, T-Pain, Beyoncé, Jermaine Dupri, 50 Cent, and Sean Garrett comprise the twenty (some appear on the list more than once).

⁶ An exception to this rule is in Nashville, where the current trend is to adhere to the contemporary sound. So much so, that at the time of this writing, the majority of country artists use the same players in the studio, regardless of whom they write, perform, and tour with.

⁷ Anthony Freud, American Voices Festival Panel, The Kennedy Center, Washington, DC, November 23–24, 2013.

⁸ *Work for hire* generally means that in exchange for a fee, the paid party is relinquishing all future rights and payments.

⁹ The American Federation of Musicians (AFM) and the Screen Actors Guild–American Federation of Television and Radio Artists (SAG-AFTRA) are labor unions representing musicians, singers, and performers in their live, televised, recorded, and other commercial work.

¹⁰ E-mail correspondence, June 27, 2013.

¹¹ E-mail correspondence, December 18, 2013.

Chapter Eleven

¹ A quick Google Image search for "Pro Tools screen shots" will show you what a typical music software session looks like. The same goes for all of the studio setups, tools, and equipment we'll be speaking about in this section.

² The construction and sonic characteristics of studios are critical to the quality of recordings. Rooms are designed, for example, to have no right angles or parallel surfaces so as to prevent sound reflection; expensive sonic absorbing panels and materials keep ambient sound from interfering with the recording process.

³ E-mail correspondence, July 9, 2013.

⁴ E-mail correspondence, September 27, 2007.

⁵ Some of the more popular companies that make microphones include Neumann, AKG, M-Audio, Sontronics, Lauten, Shure, and Audio Technica.

⁶ A *preamplifier* is an electronic device that prepares a signal for further amplification. We'll be talking in detail about frequency, EQ, compression, and limiting in the next chapter.

⁷ E-mail correspondence, July 9, 2013.

⁸ Mark Casstevens, cited from Cal Newport's *So Good They Can't Ignore You* (New York, NY: Grand Central Publishing, 2012).

⁹ E-mail correspondence, March 7, 2014.

¹⁰ The music for "Misty" was composed by Erroll Garner in 1954, with lyrics added by Johnny Burke in 1955. "Over the Rainbow" was written by Harold Arlen and E. Y. Harburg for the 1939 movie *The Wizard of Oz*.

Chapter Twelve

¹ Here's a more detailed explanation than the one in Chapter Nine of how to use speakers with little to no bleed: run a mono mix into a pair of speakers that are both aimed

precisely at the microphone, exactly the same distance from it at exactly the same angle in relation to it. The angle doesn't matter, so long as they're mirror images from the microphone's point of view. Then, reverse the wires on the back of one of the speakers. This will create an out-of-phase mix that will effectively cancel itself out at the microphone if it's been set up correctly, leaving very little to no bleed on the vocal track.

[2] Headphones come in closed-back, semi-open, and open-back models.

[3] E-mail correspondence, June 27, 2013.

[4] An exception is wind instrumentalists, who often struggle with the same issues.

[5] Matt Engstrom, "Understanding Headphone and Earphone Specifications," YouTube: www.youtube.com/watch?v=5MWk7jejhxQ, May 22, 2013.

[6] It is important for vocalists to have their hearing checked periodically, particularly those having trouble in the studio or onstage using in-ear monitors, as it is often a culprit in seemingly technical issues.

[7] David Mellor, "EQ: How and When to Use It: Tips and Techniques," *Sound on Sound* magazine, March 1995.

[8] Also related to compression is a *noise gate*, which is essentially the opposite of a limiter. Whereas a limiter limits how loud a note can get, the gate limits how quiet it can be by filtering out sounds below a certain volume threshold.

[9] E-mail correspondence, June 29, 2013.

[10] The record was "Peg o' My Heart" by Harmonicats, released in 1947. Digital reverb came along in the 1970s.

[11] Walt Disney's *Fantasia* (1940) was the first commercial motion picture to use stereo sound.

[12] E-mail correspondence, June 29, 2013.

[13] Digital perfectionism is just as common in acoustic music, where a tremendous amount of editing is often done to even the sparsest of arrangements.

[14] Masterly Singing Series: A Master Class and Conversation with Dawn Upshaw, The Metropolitan Opera, March 3, 2013.

[15] E-mail correspondence, December 20, 2013.

[16] *Lo* and *hi* are technical shorthand for low and high (and the way the terms are often labeled on gear and in technical manuals). As well, "lo and hi" generally refer to frequency, while "low and high" generally refer to level, or volume.

[17] *kHz*, or kilohertz, are thousands of Hertz (aka, the number of Hertz multiplied by one thousand).

[18] *Gain* refers to volume or level.

[19] Björgvin Benediktsson, "7 Motivational Quotes from Recording Experts That Will Kickstart Your Musical Inspiration," www.audio-issues.com, retrieved March 1, 2015.

[20] Craig Anderton, "Audio Mastering In Your Computer: How to Achieve Classy-Sounding Results," *Sound on Sound* magazine, August 2004.

Chapter Thirteen

[1] Given our focus on technology, we'll be primarily discussing commercial live performance.

[2] Even when you're on an entirely self-contained tour, venue staff and local crew members will usually be present, certainly in those spaces where the stagehand unions require it.

[3] Andrew Kania, "Making Tracks: The Ontology of Rock Music," *Journal of Aesthetics and Art Criticism*, Volume 64, Issue 4, pages 401–414, Fall 2006.

[4] Thanks to advances in storage and memory capabilities, today many of those computers are laptops, even in some of the most high-profile gigs.

[5] The first use of stage front monitors was purportedly at a 1961 Judy Garland concert in California. Other sources claim that they were first used in 1965 when the Beatles performed at Shea Stadium.

[6] E-mail correspondence, February 5, 2014.

[7] E-mail correspondence, March 2, 2010.

[8] Joan Lader interview, Fall Voice Conference, NYU School of Medicine, October 4–6, 2012.

[9] Quote from "Music and the Brain---Music, Inspiration, and Creativity: Does Practice Make Perfect?" with Daniel J. Levitin with Victor Wooten, 92nd Street Y, New York, NY, November 3, 2010.

[10] www.askdrsears.com/topics/parenting/discipline-behavior/discipline-for-children, retrieved August 13, 2015. Dr. Sears is actually a pediatrician, and this quote is from one of his books on discipline. Still, I find it to be equally important in the singing realm. Like most wisdom, the gems travel.

[11] Henry Rollins, *Black Coffee Blues* (Los Angeles, CA: 2.13.61 Publishing, 1997).

Chapter Fourteen

[1] Retrieved August 2, 2015: www.rosssimmonds.com.

[2] Don Miguel Ruiz Jr., *The Five Levels of Attachment: Toltec Wisdom for the Modern World* (San Antonio, TX: Hierophant Publishing, 2015), 16.

[3] Hillary Rodham Clinton, *Living History* (New York, NY: Scribner, 2004).

[4] Nancy Lloyd, "Deepak Chopra Walks the Walk of Spirituality," *Los Angeles Times*, www.latimes.com/health/la-he-5q-chopra-20141213-story.html, retrieved December 15, 2014.

[5] Wilson Mizner, to a San Francisco newspaper, July 5, 1932.

[6] Silvia Nakkach, *Free Your Voice: Awaken to Life Through Singing* (Louisville, CO: Sounds True, 2012), 57.

[7] Personal conversation, April 12, 2012.

[8] Personal conversation, May 13, 2013.

[9] "It's Not Right But It's Okay," written by F. Jerkins III, L. Daniels, R. Jerkins, from the album *My Love Is Your Love*, Arista Records, 1998.

[10] Robert Safian, "Twelve Innovation Lessons for 2014," *Fast Company* magazine, March 2014.

Chapter Fifteen

[1] H. Jackson Brown Jr., *P.S. I Love You* (New York: NY, Rutledge Hill Press, 1990), 9.

[2] Allison Moorer on *World Café*, NPR, April 27, 2011.

[3] Thomas Friedman, "How to Get a Job at Google," *New York Times*, February 22, 2014.

[4] Farrah Gray, *Get Real, Get Rich: Conquer the 7 Lies Blocking You from Success* (New York, NY: Dutton Adult: 2007), xii.

Index